Alexander Gregg, Charles Gillette

A few historic records of the church in the diocese of Texas, during the rebellion : together with a correspondence between the Right Rev. Alexander Gregg and the Rev. Charles Gillette

Alexander Gregg, Charles Gillette

A few historic records of the church in the diocese of Texas, during the rebellion : together with a correspondence between the Right Rev. Alexander Gregg and the Rev. Charles Gillette

ISBN/EAN: 9783337208059

Printed in Europe, USA, Canada, Australia, Japan

Cover: Foto ©ninafisch / pixelio.de

More available books at **www.hansebooks.com**

A FEW

HISTORIC RECORDS OF THE CHURCH

IN THE

Diocese of Texas,

DURING THE REBELLION.

TOGETHER WITH A

CORRESPONDENCE

BETWEEN THE

Right Rev. ALEXANDER GREGG, D.D.,

AND THE

Rev. CHARLES GILLETTE,

RECTOR OF ST. DAVID'S, AUSTIN.

New-York:
JOHN A. GRAY & GREEN, PRINTERS, 16 AND 18 JACOB STREET.
1865.

PREFACE.

In giving the following pages to the public, it may be proper to state that I am influenced by two motives: a defence of my own rights, and the rights of Presbyters and Deacons, and a defence of the Church against the usurpations of one of her highest ministers. I conceive that in the following discussion very grave principles, involving the liberty of conscience, and the freedom of Presbyters and Deacons to exercise it, and also the usages and teachings of the Church in this particular, are specially trenched upon by the Bishop.

It is with a view of bringing this matter before the Church at large, that, if possible, the question may be settled by such alterations of the law as may make the duty of each order of the ministry plain, that I make the following correspondence public. If a Bishop has a right to introduce prayers into the service of the Church on all occasions of public worship, and keep them there for years, then the Constitution and Canons of the Church need revising, so as to state the fact; and if a Bishop has a right to introduce a mere political opinion into a prayer, by way of simple assertion, by authority of the Church, and to exclude from the exercise of their office all his clergy who do not agree with him, and cannot make the assertion with a good conscience, then the Church herself needs reform.

HISTORIC RECORDS.

The following brief note of the Bishop, together with the extracts from his address to the Convention, and the action of the Convention, will explain themselves. The Convention was held at the city of Austin, the capital of Texas, in the month of April, 1861:

To the Clergy and Laity of the Protestant Episcopal Church in the Diocese of Texas:

DEAR BRETHREN: In compliance with the request of the Convention of the Diocese, which met in St. David's Church, Austin, on Thursday, the eleventh instant, the following extract from my address, with the action of the Convention thereon, is herewith communicated to you. This request was made at my own suggestion, that you might be saved from misapprehension on the subject, through incorrect or exaggerated statements:

EXTRACT FROM BISHOP'S ADDRESS.

"I have very recently received from the Right Rev. Leonidas Polk, D.D., Bishop of Louisiana, and the Right Rev. Stephen Elliot, Jr., D.D., Bishop of Georgia, a communication, which they have been induced to make as the Senior Bishops in the Confederate States, proposing a Convention at Montgomery, Alabama, on third July next, to be composed of the Bishops of the said Dioceses, and of three Clerical and three Lay Deputies from each, to be appointed by their respective diocesan Conventions. The object of this Convention will be, to consult upon such matters as may have arisen out of the changes in our civil affairs; and especially, as touching the relations of the Dioceses within the Confederate States to the Protestant Episcopal Church in the United States.

"It is thought better, in the language of the said communication, 'that these relations should be arranged by the common consent of all the Dioceses within the Confederate States than by the independent action of each Diocese. The one will probably lead to harmonious action, the other might produce inconvenient diversity.'

"The necessity for such consultation, it is further added, 'does not arise out of any dissension which has occurred within the Church itself, nor out of any dissatisfaction with either the doctrine or discipline of the Church. We rejoice to record the fact, that we are to-day, as Churchmen, as truly brethren as we have ever been, and that no deed has been done, nor word uttered, which leaves a single wound rankling in our hearts; we are still one in faith, in purpose, and in hope. But, political changes, forced upon us by a stern necessity, have occurred, which have placed our Dioceses in a position requiring consultation as to our future ecclesiastical relations.'

"As to what is here said respecting its essential unity, and the spirit of peace and concord prevailing in the Church, to this day, all must agree. Of the propriety, too, of such consultation, at this grave juncture in our ecclesiastical as well as civil history, it appears to me no doubt should be entertained; and I heartily concur in the recommendation here made. It will devolve upon this body, if it should agree in this opinion, to take the action proposed.

"If there are elements of change which can not be overruled or controlled, a fraternal interchange of views and harmonious action will doubtless give to these changes a right direction.

"If again, the general sentiment of the Church, North and South, should ultimately be found to tend to the expediency of a severance of the ecclesiastical union heretofore existing, then friendly consultation on our part, as preparatory to the final action of the General Convention, would be every way desirable.

"Or, if there may be ecclesiastically a union, as there is unquestionably, in doctrine and feeling, a unity of the Church Catholic, which is above all nationalities, the course here suggested, under the peculiar circumstances in which we are placed, will be most likely to lead to its recognition.

"And if, in accordance with this latter view, though our present ecclesiastical organization should have to give way to the force of circumstances, another should be established, providing, as a bond of union, for a General Council of the Church in all the States, to meet once in six years, or at longer intervals of time, and legislate on matters affecting the Church in its Catholicity, as its Liturgy and Faith, with Provincial Synods, composed of Dioceses contiguous and naturally falling together, meeting once in three years, to take charge of their missionary and other local work—the annual Diocesan Conventions assembling, of course, as heretofore—an end would have been attained most important in the consequences resulting from the spectacle of such a union for the Church and the world, as well as in the happy effects directly upon the great body of the faithful—an end for which the mind of the Church seems to have been gradually preparing, and which many earnest hearts have longed to bring about.

"May every change be directed aright, and the course of this world so peaceably ordered by God's governance, that His Church may joyfully serve him in all godly quietness, through Jesus Christ our Lord."

ACTION OF THE CONVENTION.

Friday, April 12.—On motion of the Rev. B. Eaton, that part of the Bishop's Address relating to a Convention of Dioceses in the Confederate States, to be held at Montgomery, Alabama, on the third day of July next, was referred to a special committee.

The Bishop appointed the Rev. Messrs. Eaton, Gillette, and Rucker, and Messrs. W. P. H. Douglass and W. L. Robards said committee.

Saturday, April 13.—The Rev. B. Eaton and the Rev. L.

P. Rucker having presented majority and minority reports from said committee,

On motion of the Rev. L. H. Jones, it was

Resolved, That, in accordance with the recommendation of the Bishop, this Convention send three clerical and three lay deputies to the proposed Convention at Montgomery.

Resolved, As the sense of this Convention, that the action of the said proposed Convention be returned to the Convention of this Diocese for ratification or rejection.

The Rev. Messrs. Eaton, Gillette, and Jones, and Messrs. P. W. Gray, S. M. Swenson, and A. M. Lewis were elected deputies.

You will perceive, from the foregoing, the reasons for this movement at the present time.

Before the last of June, the Conventions of all the Dioceses within the Confederate States will have met.

And it was foreseen that, unless joint action, as in the proposed Convention at Montgomery, should be agreed upon, there would be independent Diocesan action, leading to inconvenient diversity, and to a severance, moreover, of those bonds which have united us so long, and so happily, with our Northern brethren.

What the result of this general consultation will be can not be foreseen. Whatever action may be taken will be marked by calmness, moderation, and a spirit of peace and love.

If it can be made to appear that some bond of union may continue to exist, as suggested in my Address, it will be ground of rejoicing.

The thought of a violent rending of the Church, or of a separation, if such must needs be, otherwise than as brethren and friends, is not for a moment to be entertained. We bless God for the spectacle of union and of unity which the Protestant Episcopal Church in this country has ever presented to the world.

And, whatever its future history may be, we feel assured it will be only such as we would desire to see written.

Peace on earth and good will toward men, will be, as of old, the message proclaimed.

You will join me, I know, in fervent prayers to God that His good Spirit may be with us in our councils, and that His Church may be one; evermore preserving the unity of the Spirit in the bond of peace.

ALEX. GREGG, Bishop of Texas.

AUSTIN, April 15, 1861.

The following are the majority and minority reports presented, and referred to in the preceding minutes. The majority report was rejected only by the Bishop's giving the casting vote:

MAJORITY REPORT.

We, the undersigned, to whom was referred that part of the Bishop's Address relative to the anticipated meeting of a Convention at Montgomery, consisting of delegates from the Dioceses of the Confederate States, have had the same under consideration, and, after mature deliberation, recommend the accompanying resolutions for adoption:

1. *Resolved*, That the Diocese of Texas, in Convention assembled, repudiate the idea that the dissolution of the civil government necessarily involves a division of ecclesiastical organization; but shall at all times oppose any effort to change the same, or connect the Diocese with any body or association not first recognized and approved by the General Convention of the Protestant Episcopal Church of America.

2. *Resolved*, That we regard the assembling of a Convention, composed of only the Dioceses of the Confederate States, recommended by the Rt. Rev. Bishops Polk and Elliot, and referred to in the Address of our Bishop, as premature, and calculated to disturb the present harmony of the Church; and we do hereby solemnly protest against the separate or connected action of said Dioceses affecting our ecclesiastical position, previous to the assembling of the General Convention.

3. *Resolved*, That as the Church has always avoided politics, and especially the agitation of questions growing out of our domestic institutions, we have great confidence in the

sound conservative feeling in the Church, North as well as South, and should deeply regret to see any action which would weaken our bonds of ecclesiastical union.

4. *Resolved*, That we have cherished fond hopes concerning the permanent establishment of the University of the South; and as the Dioceses of Tennessee and North-Carolina are specially identified with us in the accomplishment of this great work, we should, at least, desire their coöperation before taking any step which would cause a change in our Church relations.

5. *Resolved*, That while we entertain the sentiment contained in the foregoing resolutions, and desire that no action should be had, yet a Convention of the Dioceses of the Confederate States may assemble; we therefore recommend the election of three clerical and three lay delegates, to meet in said Convention, with instructions to oppose to the utmost any effort to disturb our present ecclesiastical union, or the formation of any other, with powers inconsistent with the Constitution and Canons of the Protestant Episcopal Church in America.

13th April, 1861.

BENJ. EATON,
CHARLES GILLETTE,
W. P. H. DOUGLASS,
W. L. ROBARDS.

MINORITY REPORT.

The undersigned, one of the Committee to whom was referred so much of the Bishop's Address as related to the proposed Convention at Montgomery, Ala., dissenting from the report agreed upon by said Committee, begs leave to submit the following minority report:

Whereas, The Senior Bishops of the Confederate States have recommended a General Convention of the Dioceses comprised within the Confederate States, to meet at Montgomery, Ala., on the third of July next, to take into consideration the changes necessary to be made in our ecclesiastical relations growing out of the new civil relations in which we have been placed by "the powers that be."

And whereas, This Convention recognizes the principle set forth in the Canons of the primitive Church, and so earnestly contended for by the Protestant Fathers of our truly Catholic and Apostolic Church, as opposed to the assumed universal authority of the Papacy, namely, that, in every separate national civil government, the Church should be *independent* and *free* from all foreign ecclesiastical jurisdiction.

And whereas, For the purposes of harmony and uniformity, it is important that whatever changes may be made, either in the doctrines, discipline, or worship of the Church, should be done by all the Dioceses concerned acting in concert; therefore,

Resolved, 1, That the Convention concurs with the recommendation of the Senior Bishops of the Confederate States in the expediency of the proposed Convention at Montgomery, Ala., on the third of July next.

Resolved, 2, That the Convention elect delegates, as proposed, to attend said Convention without instructions.

Resolved, 3, That the action of said Convention at Montgomery, Ala., should not be considered final in this Diocese, until ratified and approved by our Diocesan Convention duly convened.

April 13th, 1861. L. P. RUCKER.

In June, 1861, Bishop Gregg issued the following prayer, to be used in the Diocese during the continuance of the war:

PRAYER.

"O most powerful and glorious Lord God! the Lord of Hosts, that rulest and commandest all things: Thou sittest in the throne judging right, and therefore we make our address to thy Divine Majesty in this our necessity, that thou wouldest take the cause into thy own hand, and judge between us and our enemies.

"Stir up thy strength, O Lord! and come and help us; for thou givest not always the battle to the strong, but canst save by many or by few.

"Give wisdom, courage, and every needful virtue to those chosen leaders, who may conduct our armies on the field of strife; preserve them all from vain glorying, and from every undue excess in the hour of victory; and especially be with those who have gone, or may go forth in defense of their homes, of the institutions transmitted to them, and of every cherished right. Save them from the temptations to which they may be exposed, guard them from danger, strengthen and support them in the discharge of every duty to their country, and to thee, O Lord! God of our fathers! the rock of our refuge, who wilt give, we humbly trust, to thy injured people, victory at the last. We thank thee for the tokens of thy favor already vouchsafed. Continue them, we beseech thee, as we do put our trust in thee; and grant that the unnatural war which has been forced upon us, may speedily be brought to a close, in the deliverance of thy people, in the restoration of peace, in the strengthening of our Confederate Government, that it may continue to flourish and prosper; and in the advancement of thy glory, O blessed Lord God! who dost live and govern all things, world without end, through Jesus Christ our Lord. AMEN."

Although I thought this prayer savored by far too strong of party feeling for public use in the Church, yet I could conscientiously use all the petitions, feeling that if it was God's will that they should be granted, I might well cry: "Thy will, O God! be done." But when it came to the mere assertion of a fact, about which the Almighty was certainly better informed than any man could be, and concerning which there was great difference of opinion—an assertion which I did not believe to be true, as a matter of fact—I did not think it to be right for me to make it. It so happened that for a week or two after the prayer was put forth, either the Bishop or some other clergyman was with me, and took the part of the service in which the prayer occurred. During this time I took occasion to speak with the Bishop, stating some of my objections to the use of the words, and especially my disbelief of what they asserted. I observed that they might be omitted without affecting in the slightest degree any petition in the prayer; and asked him to give me permission to omit them when I used the prayer. At the time, the Bishop said their insertion was not in accordance with the usage of the Church, and on this ground he would have left them out of the prayer, if it had been pointed out to him before the prayer was printed. He, however, gave me permission to omit the words—a permission which I understood at the time to be as lasting as the use of the prayer; and in my case, to extend to any place in the Diocese. In this, it afterward appeared, I was very much mistaken. The Bishop felt compelled first to limit me to my own parish, and afterward to withdraw the permission altogether. In regard to limiting me to my own parish, he evidently assumed an authority which is nowhere granted to him by canon. The law under which he put forth the prayer—which is the only one relating to the subject—enjoins a clergyman to use the prayer for an extraordinary occasion, only in his "accustomed place of worship." If I had been traveling, therefore, in any part of the Diocese, during the four years of the continuance of the war, I should have felt under no obligation, by the law of the Church, to have used the Bishop's prayer on any occasion of public worship outside of my own parish. Therefore, when the Bishop forbade my officiating outside of my parish, unless I used, not only the prayer, but the words he had given me permission to omit, he certainly went beyond his authority.

In 1862, the Convention of the Diocese of Texas met in Houston. I extract from the Journal, as follows:

On motion of Rev. Mr. Dalzell,

"*Resolved*, That so much of the Episcopal Address as refers to our relation to the Confederate States, and to the Church in the United States, be referred to a special committee.

"The following were appointed such Committee: Rev. W. T. D. Dalzell, Rev. John Owen, Major S. Maclin, Colonel J. B. Hawkins, and Colonel A. M. Lewis."

"The Committee to whom was referred that portion of the Bishop's Address, having reference to the relation of the Church in this Diocese to the Confederate States, and also to the Protestant Episcopal Church in the United States, have given the subject that careful attention which its great importance demands, and beg to submit the following report:

"In the first place, the Committee feel that the Church in

this Diocese has cause of thankfulness in the course adopted at the last Convention, when, in response to the Circular Letter from the two Senior Bishops then within the Confederate States, delegates were elected to represent this Diocese in the Convention which assembled at Montgomery, in July last: because, although no one of the Delegates elected was able to attend that Convention, the action of this Diocese having been concurrent with that of every other Diocese within the Confederacy, is evidence that we had adopted a principle of action approved by the Bishops, Clergy, and Laity of the Church, as being catholic in its nature, and the only principle by which we could be governed in the circumstances in which the Church then found herself placed in relation to the State. This principle has since then been further approved by the Churches in those States which have joined the Confederate States since our last Convention was held. And, in addition to this, the Committee also feel that the progress of events during the past year, has made it still further evident that the course pursued at the last Convention was wise, and, as we trust, directed by the great Head of the Church. The idea on which our action was based, was that an *actual* separation of certain States from the United States *had* taken place, and that a new nation having been thus established, it became necessary at least to consider, whether the Churches in the Dioceses within that new nation were not called upon, both in conformity with catholic usage in all ages of the Church, and in harmony with the system on which the Church in the United States is herself organized, to form themselves into an independent National Church. The events of the last year show that this idea was correct; that no future connection *can* exist between the States in the Confederacy and the United States; and that, not merely in order to conform with the spirit and action of the Church Catholic from the Apostolic age down to the present time, but also that the Church might be enabled to *exist at all*, and fulfill the commission conferred on her by Christ, within these Confederate States, she *must* sever her connection in so far as government and discipline are involved, with the Protestant Episcopal Church in the United States, and organize into a permanent, distinct, National Church. But the Committee would suggest that pains be taken to impress the important truth on the minds of the members of the Church, and others, within the Diocese, that in thus organizing a National Church we sever none of the *bonds of unity* that unite us in the communion of saints with the Church in the United States, and all other Churches with whom we were in communion previous to the changes which have led to our national existence.

"Secondly. The Committee would place on record the heart-felt sympathy of the Church in this Diocese with the cause of our country; our sense of the grievous wrongs which led the Southern States to separate from the Old Union; our hearty concurrence in the separation; our repudiation in behalf of our country of the charge of having initiated the present unholy war, waged against us by the United States; our deep and abiding conviction that our cause is just and righteous; that the war is *forced* upon us by our enemies in defense of all the principles which the United States themselves (as Colonies) asserted, and fought for, and established, namely, the independence of each separate State (then a Colony) and its inherent right to self-government; and our solemn pledge, that our prayers shall be unceasingly offered to God for the Confederate Government, that it may continue to flourish and prosper, while, as an individual, each member of the Church will do all that lies in his power to aid and further the cause.

"The Committee further desire to express concurrence in the action of the Convention held at Montgomery and Columbia; a concurrence, however, which has been already shown by this Convention, in its adoption of the Proposed Permanent Constitution for the Church in the Confederate States, set forth by the Convention at Columbia.

"In order, regularly and forcibly to express the sentiments here recorded, the Committee beg to offer to this Convention the following resolutions, for adoption:

"1st. *Resolved*, That this Convention now formally declare—which, in consequence of the course of events in the State, has been practically the case ever since the adjournment of the last Convention—that the Protestant Episcopal Church, in the Diocese of Texas, has ceased to be a Diocese of the Protestant Episcopal Church in the United States.

"2d. *Resolved*, That in thus declaring our independence of the Protestant Episcopal Church in the United States, this Convention simply adopts a principle of catholic usage, the application of which in our case is rendered necessary by the secession of the State of Texas from the United States— that principle being the existence of a National Church in every separate nation—while we retain the essential elements of unity with the Holy Catholic Church throughout the world.

"3d. *Resolved*, That this Convention approve of the course of the Bishop of this Diocese, and also that of the Standing Committee, in their official action since the last Convention, by which they asserted the independence of this Diocese of the Protestant Episcopal Church in the United States; and

"*Resolved further*, That this Convention heartily concur in the sentiments of the Bishop expressed in his address, and earnestly press upon the attention of the members of the Church, that portion especially which refers to their personal dangers and duties in the present crisis.

"4th. *Resolved*, That the Church in the Diocese of Texas owes civil allegiance to the Government of the Confederate States of America; that she recognizes the divine command to *submit to every ordinance of man for the Lord's sake*, and adopts the practice of the Church in all ages, in yielding allegiance to the Government of the nation in which the providence of God has placed her; while, moreover, she sympathizes heartily with the cause of the Confederate States, and prays, and will pray to God, to bring to a speedy close the unholy war which has been forced upon us, and to strengthen the Government, that it may continue to flourish and prosper.

"5th. *Resolved*, In order that the members of the Church in Texas may fully understand the present position of this Diocese, and the duties which devolve upon us in the present great emergency, the clergy are hereby requested to read to their congregations, after morning service, on the first Sunday after receiving printed copies of the Journal of this Convention, all those portions of the Bishop's Address which refer to the same, adding such remarks as they may deem expedient.

W. T. D. DALZELL, Chairman.
JOHN OWEN,
SACKFIELD MACLIN,
J. B. HAWKINS,
A. M. LEWIS,
} Members of Committee."

On motion of General Bee,

"*Resolved,* That the report and resolutions of the 'Committee to whom was referred that portion of the Bishop's Address having reference to the relation of the Church in this Diocese, to the Confederate States, and also to the Protestant Episcopal Church in the United States,' this day unanimously adopted as the sense of this Convention, be read before all the Churches of this Diocese at the time specified therein for reading so much of the Bishop's Address as refers to the subject."

It will thus be seen that to the assertion of Bishop Gregg, "this unnatural war, which was forced upon us," was added the solemn resolve of the Diocese of Texas, proclaiming the truth of the assumption. And that no doubt might any longer remain upon the minds of those who differed about the "historical fact," the proceeding, by which it was settled, was ordered to be read from every pulpit in the State. As no new argument or proof was offered, there still remained some who thought it a mere matter of judgment, and not an authoritative decree. The Convention at which the above action was taken, met on the fifth of June, 1862. I was not present at the meeting.

On Saturday, the fifth day of July, I met the Bishop on the street in the city of Austin. He inquired if I had received a copy of the Journal of the Convention, to which I replied that I had. He asked me if I observed the resolution requesting the reading of the report of the Committee on the Bishop's Address, and the resolutions. I answered that I had observed it. He then inquired if I intended to read them the following day? I told him I did not, giving as my reason that it was communion Sunday; that there was a good deal of feeling in the congregation, many supposing, as I did myself, that the

2

resolutions, and the request to read them, was directed specially against myself; that if I read them, on that day, probably a number of the communicants would leave the church; that I did not see any thing special to be gained by reading them a week earlier or later, and that I thought the following Sunday would do just as well.

The Bishop seemed much displeased, and told me, in a manner not at all pleasant, that if I would not read them the following day, he thought he would go and read them to my congregation. I was not prepared for such a proposition, made in such a way, and I replied he had no right to do that. He contended he had. After some further conversation, in which the Bishop still insisted that he had the right to read the resotions to my congregation without my consent, in virtue of its being his parish church—by which I supposed he meant the place where his family, and he, when at home, worshiped—we parted. He left me so much in doubt as to what he intended to do, that I addressed him the following note on the afternoon of the same day. I thought the Bishop was taking a stand, ignoring my rights as a presbyter, and I at once determined that, under no circumstances, should he read the resolutions the following day. I should have remarked that before we parted, I had told him that if the proceedings were read, I should not have the communion, although I had given notice for it the week previous.

Let the correspondence which followed explain itself:

"My Dear Bishop: Will you please inform me this evening what course you have determined to pursue to-morrow?

"Allow me to suggest an examination of the VI. Sec. of Can. 12, Title I. of the Digest. I take minister, as there used, to include a Bishop, except when making his visitation, as elsewhere directed in the canons. If you think I am wrong, please inform me.   Very respectfully, yours,
"Austin, July 5, 1862.   Charles Gillette."

"Austin, July 5, 1862.
"Dear Brother Gillette: I have concluded to let matters take the course to-morrow which you suggest. I have not

hitherto, nor do I now understand Sec. VI. of Can. 12, Title I., as applying to the Bishop of a Diocese. It appears to me the point alluded to would have to be determined upon other authority. Yours, truly, ALEX'R GREGG.
"Rev. C. GILLETTE."

In the following Convention, which met in June, 1863, no public action was taken in regard to myself; but soon after its adjournment I was surprised at receiving the following letter:

"HOUSTON, May 9, 1863.

"REV. AND DEAR BROTHER: You no doubt can but know that we, Presbyters in this Diocese, are aware of the position in which you are placed by the omission of the words in the Bishop's Prayer, 'which has been forced upon us.'

"Moved by the kindest feelings and a due consideration of your long residence in this Diocese, we most affectionately say to you, that your course, as above mentioned, has presented a stumbling-block to many members of the Church in our Diocese, and especially to the clergy.

"We affectionately beg, therefore, that you will endeavor to conform to the use of the omitted words in the Bishop's Prayer, so as to remove this obstacle to the harmony and unity of the Church and clergy in the Diocese of Texas.

"If this is not practicable, your brethren would kindly ask, if there is not a way of removing this difficulty, that will accord with your feelings and sentiments, and with the peace, honor, and quietness of our beloved Church in this Diocese?

"Please take the above into consideration, and reply to the Secretary of the Presbyters.

L. P. RUCKER, President.
EDWIN A. WAGNER, W. T. DICKINSON DALZELL,
S. D. DAVENPORT, R. S. SEELY.
JOHN OWEN, Secretary of the Clergy."

I did not know the meaning of this formidable body of Presbyters, to whose Secretary I was directed to make answer. A self-constituted body, coming between the Bishop and one of his clergy, in a matter which was all vested in the Bishop, and so calling a brother to an account in a matter with which they properly had nothing to do—all this seemed to me so irregular and unchurchlike, that I hardly knew what course to pursue. But, upon reflection, I thought it better to make no reply. And, accordingly, I remained silent. I have since learned that this letter was so arranged that some boasted that there was no Presbyter present who would dare refuse to sign it. But in this there was a mistake. Some had enough of the spirit of the Church to defy the political fury and refuse to sign the letter of "the Presbyters." I might not think it necessary to give this letter here if it did not make a connected link in the continued and systematic persecution, for opinion's sake, to which, for a series of years, I have been subjected. One of two things was evidently determined upon by "the Presbyters," as well as by the Bishop. Either I must give up conscience or leave the Diocese. The former I could not, and the latter would have been very difficult for me under the circumstances.

In June, 1864, the Council assembled again at Houston. As the letter of "the Presbyters" had produced no result, it became necessary for something further to be done. Accordingly, the Council took the following action:

"The following preamble and resolution was presented by the Rev. Mr. Owen:

"*Whereas*, In the severe and bloody conflicts in which our beloved country is still engaged, it is expedient and necessary that all, in and out of the Church, should be united, harmonious, and unflinching in the maintenance of our righteous cause; and whereas, in the special prayer prepared by our Bishop for the present war an historical fact is incidentally inculcated and appropriately introduced, which can not, with good reason be questioned, namely, that the war was forced upon us, and that we were not the aggressors; and whereas, the omission of the words, 'which has been forced upon us.' on the part of any clergyman, is an evil to be deprecated as a source of discord and contention, and in its measure subversive of truth, and love, and unity, and peace; therefore, be it

"*Resolved by this Council*, That the Bishop of the Diocese be most respectfully requested to withhold from every clergyman a permission to omit the aforesaid words, and to withdraw it wherever it has been granted, and thus prevent the ignoring of so important an established fact, which indubitably justifies our right to resist, even unto death, the wicked invasion of the relentless, cruel, and blood-thirsty enemies of our country.

"After some debate, the preamble and resolution were made the special order for four o'clock P.M., to which hour the Council then took a recess.

"Four o'clock P.M.—Council reässembled. Present, in addition to those in the morning, Dr. Thomas J. Heard, of St. Paul's Church, Washington.

"The preamble and resolution of Rev. Mr. Owen, being the special order for this hour, were taken up, and after some further debate, a vote by orders was called for by the Rev. Mr. Rucker, which, being duly seconded, resulted as follows:

OF THE CLERGY.

"*Ayes*—Rev. Messrs. Rucker, Owen, Seely, Davenport, and Kay.

"*Noes*—Rev. Messrs. Goshorn and Richardson.

OF THE LAITY.

"*Ayes*—St. Mark's Church, San Antonio; St. Paul's Church, Washington; St. Peter's Church, Brenham; Trinity Church, Galveston; Calvary Church, Richmond; Christ Church, Matagorda.

"*Divided*—Christ Church, Houston.

"*Excused*—Grace Church, Independence.

"On motion of Hon. C. W. Buckley, the Secretary was requested to give the Bishop a certified copy of the preamble and resolution."

This action of the Council led to the final withdrawal of the permission formerly given to omit the words, "which has been forced upon us," by the issuing of a pastoral in the latter part of June, 1864, and a short note to myself, both of which will be introduced in their proper place in the following correspondence.

After the action of the Convention in 1862, and the conversation had with the Bishop, I felt that such injustice had been done me, both by the Convention and the Bishop, that I desired to set myself right, if possible, at least with the Bishop. The Rev. Mr. Wagner, being on a visit at the Bishop's, in Austin, I desired a conference in connection with some matters which had transpired. I wished this conference in writing; but it so happened that it took place at the vestry-room of St. David's Church, the Bishop, Rev. Messrs. Wagner and Brown, and myself, being present. In the conversation, Mr. Wagner was understood to say, that the action of the Convention in 1862, in the resolutions passed, and requested to be read in each congregation, was had with a view of making me define my position, politically. This, together with other propositions, clearly made or implied in the course of the conversation, led me, a few days afterward, to draw off the ten following propositions to which I could not assent, which I submitted to the Bishop in writing, and to which he made the reply annexed:

PROPOSITIONS.

"In the conversation had with yourself and Messrs. Wagner and Brown, at the vestry-room of St. David's, on Tuesday, the fifth instant, I stated, in the beginning, that I did not expect to argue the questions involved, but only desired to get a clear statement of certain points; but that I should be glad to argue the subject at length in writing. I therefore said very little on that occasion in answer to the propositions advanced, or the statements made.

"As, in my judgment, there are very grave and important questions involved, of vital interest not only to Mr. Brown and myself, but to the whole Church of God, and to the advancement of the cause of our Divine Master in the world, I deem it my duty to make a very plain but very respectful statement of the light in which I view some of these points.

"I premise, in the beginning, that I accuse no man of *willful* wrong; but yet I think a great and grievous wrong has been done to individuals and to the Church at large.

"1st. To begin with some of the points fully stated, or as I deem clearly inferred from the conversation. I can not assent to the proposition that a Christian minister has no right to be guided by his own conscientious convictions of duty, although those convictions may be contrary to those of many or all of his brethren. Were this so, Luther and his colaborers in the Reformation must have been forever silent, and no reformation could have dawned upon the Church. The English Church would still have been sleeping quietly in the arms of the Papacy. Transubstantiation and the sale of indulgences would still have been taught and practiced, and all the monstrous dogmas growing out of these and kindred doctrines would still have covered up and defaced the Church of God. If the above proposition were true, Galileo must have submintted to the doctors of the Church, and the true science of Astronomy must still have been unknown. A minister of God can only safely follow his own convictions of right when he has carefully and prayerfully made use of the lights he has before him.

"2d. I can not assent to the proposition, that a minister of the Gospel violates the peace of the Church, when, in his own sphere, he conscientiously performs what he believes to be his duty, in accordance with the Ritual of the Church and with the permission and sanction of his Bishop, without transgressing any law or regulation of the Church. If this were so, the peace of the Church would be constantly broken, as often as *one* man differed from another on any subject whatever. If the peace of the Church is broken, it is rather they that break it who step out of their own sphere to censure and condemn those who may differ from them in opinion, in matters where the greatest liberty of opinion is allowed.

"3d. I can not assent to the proposition that a Bishop has no right to grant permission to one, or a number of his clergy, to omit a sentence, or part of a sentence in a special prayer, put forth by himself for 'extraordinary occasions.' This would be, as I conceive, to make a Bishop infallible, and his acts, like the laws of the Medes and Persians, which altered not, though a Daniel were thrown to lions for devoutly worshiping his God.

"4th. I can not assent to the proposition that a minister is responsible for the political sentiments of his congregation, and if he can not guide and control them in politics, he had better leave them to the care of some one else. This would seem to me to place politics above religion, and the care of the state above the care of souls; and I do not find this anywhere taught in the gospels, or intimated in my ordination vow.

"5th. I can not assent to the proposition that the Council of the Church, in solemn conclave, is bound to listen to the voice of the outside world, and publicly censure a brother clergyman for what it deems a political heresy, passing a series of resolutions, and requesting them to be read in open church, thereby intending to force him to define his position, politically. This would be to make the Church a political engine, to discover by moral tortures the secret opinions of her clergy, and so expose them to the malice and persecution of unprincipled men.

"6th. I can not assent to the proposition, that the present war is one for the sake of piety, and that the very existence of morality, virtue, and religion in the South, are involved in its issue. I am not able to discover any thing involved in the struggle which makes it *par excellence* a war for godliness, or for the advancement of the Redeemer's kingdom.

"7th. I can not assent to the proposition, that the injunction of our Saviour, 'Render unto Cæsar the things which be Cæsar's,' makes it the duty of a Christian minister to harangue his people publicly or privately, to arouse in them a spirit of war and all the baser passions which must inevitably accompany such a spirit, calling our enemies vandals and an infidel host, when, in the judgment of charity, they are no more infidel or irreligious than ourselves. Such a course would, I believe, be a violation of my solemn ordination vows, wherein I promised before God " to maintain and set forward as much as in me lay, quietness, peace, and love among all Christian people, and especially among those that are or shall be committed to my charge."

"8th. I can not assent to the proposition, that our last Diocesan Council has not exceeded the usual custom of the Church in political legislation, and that there has been no teaching of the clergy beyond what was meet, considering the exigencies of the times, in relation to war and its adjuncts. I pass no censure, nor arraign any one for what has been done; I simply state that, with my views of duty as a Christian minister, I could not do the same.

"9th. I can not assent to the proposition that any man has a right to go behind the words of prayer, and judge another as to whether he prays '*ex animo.*' Of this, God alone is judge.

"10th. I can not assent to the proposition, that the special prayer now in use in this Diocese is based upon the words, 'which has been forced upon us,' and without these becomes, in effect, no prayer for the times. This would make a few words of gratuitous information to the Almighty to contain the essence of all the petitions—a proposition to which my judgment does not assent.

"I feel that the action of my brethren partakes largely of an intolerant, sectarian, and persecuting spirit; a spirit which says, 'You must think and speak as I do, or not at all;' and that, too, when no doctrine or article of faith is concerned. In feeling thus, I give every individual credit for wishing to do right; for an intolerant and persecuting spirit is compatible with the utmost sincerity. St. Paul had no greater sincerity or desire to serve God when he preached the Gospel and was himself persecuted, than when, in former times, he had persecuted the followers of Jesus, even unto strange cities and to death.

"I feel that my brethren are proposing a new test of fitness for ministerial labor among them, hitherto unknown in the Church. They are saying: 'You must believe with us politically, or you can not labor in the Church with us. We can not fraternize with you, without this; but we will, by our acts, publicly say you are unworthy to labor with us, as a minister, in the Church of God.'"

To this paper, the Bishop returned the following, as a reply:

In reply to the paper submitted by Rev. Mr. Gillette, as to conversation held between himself and Mr. Brown, on the one part, and Rev. Mr. Wagner and myself, on the other, and the matters involved, I remark, in the first place, (and wish to be understood as speaking in all candor and kindness, however plainly,) that of the ten propositions deduced by Mr. Gillette from said conversation, and from the acts of Convention and the clergy, to which he can not assent, there is, in my opinion, but *one*, the eighth, which is deducible from any thing that has been said or has occurred, and even *that* is not set forth correctly in strictness of language. But, let the propositions be taken up in order, however misapprehended, that the whole subject may be discussed.

The questions involved, both as to principle and practical consequences, are indeed grave and important for individuals and the Church, and unhappy results have already transpired; but not, I am persuaded, through the fault or error of their brethren, as to Rev. Messrs. Gillette and Brown. Of willful wrong, I trust no one is suspected. May not the present state of things, as to them, be attributable rather to erroneous opinion and position in the outset, and misconception, in consequence as to what has since occurred?

As to the first proposition, to which Mr. Gillette can not assent, " That a Christian minister has no right to be guided by his own conscientious convictions of duty, although those convictions may be contrary to the convictions of many, or all of his brethren," I do not understand it to have been made directly or indirectly. And yet, as here broadly and comprehensively stated, its converse may, in some aspects, admit of very important qualifications.

Has a clergyman, or any man, a right to be guided by conscientious convictions, unless he has taken the pains to enlighten his conscience by a well-informed judgment? Suppose, as in the case before us, these convictions are based upon a political opinion, the party entertaining them all the while *eschewing politics*, has he not reason to distrust himself? Would not common prudence dictate that he should be willing to take the opinion of the statesmen of the country, if you please, the wisest laymen of the Church; just as he would expect a politician, or man of the world, in matters of religious faith and practice, to take *counsel* of the divines of the Church?

But, granting his opinion is fixed and unchangeable—and his

conscientious convictions based thereon must be his guide—how far has a clergyman of the Church the right, in consequence thereof, to persist in a line of conduct, or in maintaining a position at war with the general sentiment and feeling of the diocese and a large part of his individual congregation, a course on his part, to a certain extent, disturbing the peace and bringing reproach on the Church, besides leading inevitably to alienations and divisions, or fostering and increasing *such feelings*, already in existence, among those committed to his charge? *Under such unhappy* circumstances, is he, of conscientious necessity, to remain where he is?

As to the second proposition to which Mr. Gillette can not assent, "That a minister of the Gospel violates the peace of the Church when, in his own sphere, he conscientiously performs what he believes to be his duty, in accordance with the ritual of the Church, and with the permission and sanction of his Bishop, and without transgressing any law or regulation of the Church," I do not understand that, in this form, any such proposition has been made; because, first, we believe the course of Rev. Mr. Gillette not to have been in accordance with the ritual of the Church, in so far, at least, as the spirit of the ritual is that of unity and peace; and second, because, though with the permission of his Bishop, he has omitted certain words in the prayer, it was by no means with the Bishop's sanction or approval, but simply a point yielded, with pain, to Mr. Gillette's conscience, and with sad apprehensions, at the time, of the results which would ensue. But, taking the proposition as it stands, it may not be untenable, for the reason that a minister *may so far err* in the *manner* of performing what he conceives to be his duty, as to violate the peace of the Church, though in letter he may not seem to violate the Church's ritual or laws.

As to the third proposition, to which Mr. Gillette can not assent, "That a bishop has no right to grant permission to one or a number of his clergy, to omit a sentence, or a part of a sentence, in a special prayer, put forth by himself for extraordinary occasions," I am not aware that it has been maintained; but, on the contrary, I understand the right referred to, to have been expressly admitted by *those* who have expressed the most decided opinion as to the inexpediency of such *permission* having been granted. Supposing, however, any to hold the proposition, as set forth by Mr. Gillette, it would by no means follow, as he intimates, that it would make the Bishop infallible, or his acts "like the laws of the Medes and Persians, which change not, though a Daniel were thrown to lions for devoutly worshiping his God." For while none, within the pale of Protestantism at least, are so weak as to entertain any such notion of a bishop's opinions or acts, yet it might, with some show of reason, be held that a bishop had no right (albeit with power, if he chose) to permit, in favor of one or more of his clergy, what would seriously affect the uniformity of prayer, and perhaps the Christian feelings and peace of the congregations of a diocese.

As to the fourth proposition to which Mr. Gillette can not assent, "That a minister is responsible for the political sentiments of his congregation, and if he can not guide and control them in politics, he had better leave them to the care of some one else," I can only express my surprise that Mr. Gillette should understand any one to have made it, and add emphatically, God forbid that it should be so; and yet, with a disavowal of the proposition as here laid down, I can readily understand how a minister may incur a serious responsibility in connection with the political sentiments of a part or the whole of his congregation—*responsible*, if not for their opinions originally, at least in giving his sanction thereto, in encouraging a line of conduct based thereon, and in arraying, it may be most defiantly, a part of the congregation against the rest. For, though professing to exclude politics *in toto* in the pulpit, and actually abstaining, in letter, from any thing of the kind, he may, notwithstanding, make himself a *decided partisan*, giving all the weight of his official influence and pastoral connection to such a course; and *so do it* that *no one* in or out of the Church will misunderstand his position. He may do it in the pulpit, throughout a great revolution and a bloody and protracted war, both in his ordinary routine and on extraordinary occasions, as of public fast or thanksgiving appointed by those in authority, by such a studied silence as to the great questions agitating the state, and the events transpiring around him, moving the hearts of millions of people, though in their spiritual bearing, as never to betray any sympathy with the government and country in their perilous struggle—a silence which he knows will be pleasing to a part, and as offensive to the other portion of his congregation—a silence which the very instincts of our nature in the love of country, as they are recognized and sanctioned by the Scriptures, would seem to forbid—a silence which ignores these special topics in their spiritual bearings, to say the least, which the times demand for the improvement of a people; *as, for example*, the temptation to the spirit of extortion, of revenge, of profanity, of reliance upon an arm of flesh and undue absorption, in short, in the things of the present, in its extraordinary character to the neglect of spiritual things, and the *duties* which every good citizen owes to the state. He *may do it* again, most emphatically, by omitting certain words in a prayer put forth by his bishop, upon which the great question in connection with the public troubles, in the judgment of many of his people, as of the laity of the Church at large, is thought to depend: namely, as to the *fact*, whether the war was forced upon us—a course on his part calculated to excite in the people more bitter feelings, than an open avowal of his sentiments in connection therewith, however adverse, at such a crisis, and calculated to lead to more unhappy consequences in the end. Again, he may show a decidedly partisan spirit, by allowing himself, for whatever reason, to cherish most, if not all his private sympathetic associations with a certain class of his congregation, and these generally supposed to be disaffected toward the government, or at least not sympathizing with the country in its struggle—a course which would be decisive of *strong political feeling and sympathy* in the judgment of mankind.

As to the fifth proposition, to which Mr. G. can not assent, " That the Council of the Church in solemn conclave is bound to listen to the voice of the outside world, and publicly censure a brother clergyman for what they deem a political heresy, passing a series of resolutions, and requesting them to be read in open church, thereby intending him to define his position politically," it certainly has not been made to my knowledge, nor is it deducible from the action of the Convention, by any process of reasoning whatever. For the proposition, as here set forth, is based upon an entire distortion of the character of the Convention, as an assemblage of the Church, as well as its motives and objects in the action referred to. It was, in no sense, a "*conclave*," but a public open meeting—its motive is to be found in the civil and ecclesiastical changes that had taken place, as its object was for the Church in this Diocese, as it ought to have done, to give a formal and solemn expression of its feelings and sentiments as to its relation to the Protestant Episcopal Church in the United States, and to the Confederate States, and *also* as to the unnatural war which is being waged against us, with the grave questions connected with it. Such a declaration, under the circumstances, was due to that government, in its present perilous struggle, to which our hearty allegiance is due. The report and resolutions of the Committee rise far above the contemplation of individuals, whose course, indeed, may have helped, in their measure, to make such action eminently proper. There is, in fact, no allusion to persons—nor any language of censure, except by implication—though there is a distinct reference to the war, in language reïterated, as " having been forced upon us." But this point had been made nearly a year before by the Rev. Mr. Gillette himself, in one of the leading parishes of the Diocese, by his declining, on grounds of conscience, to read the words, " which has been forced upon us," in the prayer put forth by the Bishop—leading, in his own parish and elsewhere throughout the Diocese, to general remark and much feeling, as was naturally to be expected. It was, in fact, an issue previously made by Mr. Gillette with his Bishop as to a point which the clergy and laity of the Church, with very few exceptions, conceive to be of vast moral consequence in connection with the present war. With him, therefore, rests the responsibility, whatever there be, of first making a distinct political issue, if it can be so called, when none had been thought of, and as was supposed, except with those anti-Southern in feelings, there could be no difference of opinion. The matter having been so much talked of and commented on throughout the Diocese, because of the extraordinary character of the issue made, and that a point touching the uniformity of prayer in the Church, it was most proper and becoming that the Convention should solemnly declare "that this unnatural war has been forced upon us," for the vindication of the Bishop, of a suffering country, of the Church's integrity, its members of all degrees having embarked their lives and fortunes in the struggle, and for its justification before God, in praying for victory over our foes. Of course, such a declaration, and that repeated, reflected seriously upon the position and course of Mr. Gillette, but it is his unhappiness, not the fault of the Convention, that such should be the case. It was the natural result of his previous course, persisted in at a time when there should be no division as to *such a question*, and contrary, as he well knew, to the general feeling and act of the Church, as expressed in prayer to God. In the language adopted by the Convention, there is no word of harshness unbecoming such a body, and nothing that savors of the excitement and vindictiveness of a political assemblage greatly roused. If there was any propriety in adopting the report and resolutions, there was certainly *as much* in requesting them to be read in all the churches of the Diocese. When matters of importance have been acted on by Conventions of the Church, in which general interest was felt by her members at large, it has not been unusual to have such actions brought before the congregations. It was eminently proper in this case, for reasons which have already been stated. It is questionable, I think, from what transpired at the time, whether there was, in the moving or adoption of the *resolutions*, any special thought of, or reference to, Mr. Gillette. It had been already resolved that *that* portion of the Episcopal Address referred to, should be read in the churches, and the other was very naturally added. The *real object*, if I understand it, was thus to have publicly made known, in all the parishes and to the Church at large, what the Convention had done; and in no other way could this object have been so effectually accomplished. There certainly can be no foundation whatever for the implied charge, that the action of the Convention "made the Church a political engine, to discover, by moral torture, the secret opinions of her clergy, and so expose them to the malice and persecution of irreligious and unprincipled men." Was this remarkable language well weighed? The Church of Christ prostituting itself to the work of exposing its own clergy to the malice and persecution of irreligious and unprincipled men? Who entertain secret opinions now? Is it *a time* for such things? If I am not mistaken, the Convention generally regarded Mr. Gillette's position, as to the war at least, as being well defined. If it had been otherwise, the mere reading the resolutions in his parish could be no defining of his position—his refusal to do so would have been significant. The Convention knew, of course, that it could only request the clergy to read, having no authority to *enforce a compliance*, and not only as to the *war*, Mr. Gillette's opinion as to our separation from the Church in the United States was well known, after the meeting of the Convention in 1861, in St. David's, and I may add as to our political separation also. What secret opinion was it, then, which the Convention would fain have extracted? Finally, as to the proposition before us, "It was no voice from the outside world to which the Convention had listened," but the cognizance of facts, well known throughout the Diocese, which shaped its action to the extent already explained.

As to the sixth proposition, to which Mr. G. can not assent, "That the present war is one for the sake of piety, and that the very existence of morality, virtue, and religion in the South, are involved in its issue," I am not aware that it has been made. It is surely a sad misconception of what has been said on the subject, to suppose it implies that this is a war "*par excellence*" for godliness or for the advancement of the Redeemer's kingdom. When or by whom has such an opinion been expressed? We do hold, with one consent, that it is a *war* in the issue of which morality and religion are involved, though not their existence, to an extent beyond that of any other war of modern times, if not beyond any since the days when the kingdoms of darkness were leagued against the infant Church of Christ for its destruction.

We do not maintain, indeed, that the war is waged on our part "*par excellence*" for godliness, but for our liberties and independence, for our cherished rights as States, and for our peculiar institution; and, in the overthrow of these—in the scenes that would precede and those which would follow, in the yoke which subjugation by our foes would impose, and the bloody horrors ever attending the efforts to throw it off—that our very religion, as we now have it and enjoy it, would be lamentably involved; passing under a dark cloud, all ecclesiastical organizations, as now existing, being broken up; and a scattered and almost exterminated people, as we would be, forced to worship the God of their fathers in secret places, in the wilderness, or mountains and caves of the earth. In this sense and to this extent we are fighting for religion, and rely upon God for deliverance.

As to the seventh proposition to which Mr. G. can not assent, "That the injunction of our Saviour, 'Render unto Cæsar the things which be Cæsar's,' makes it the duty of a Christian minister to harangue his people publicly or privately, to arouse in them a spirit of war, and all the baser passions which must inevitably accompany such a spirit, calling our enemies vandals and an infidel host, when in the judgment of charity they are no more infidel or irreligious than ourselves, I ask: Who has laid down such a proposition as a whole? What clergyman of the Church has harangued his people, as that term is generally understood, or endeavored by noisy address, in public or private, to arouse in them a spirit of war—an attempt, to say the least, that would have been quite unnecessary; that spirit having been justly roused in a people who are determined, in reliance on the help of God, to defend themselves from the invasions, ravages, and horrible purposes of an exterminating foe? I do understand, that the injunction of our Saviour referred to, imposes the duty of allegiance to the government under which we live, and of supporting it in defense of its liberties, and that this allegiance or fidelity to the state—a natural obligation, as society is formed, not less than the subject of divine injunction—is wholly incompatible with the desire, or willingness, or even indifference; that a government at war with our own, and seeking to overthrow it, should succeed in the attempt, and be reëstablished in its stead. And, furthermore, that this duty of allegiance or fidelity to the State makes it imperative on every citizen and subject thereof, in his proper sphere, and by every means becoming his character and position, to assist in the defense of his country and its institutions, and, so far as he can, to guide and encourage those who are nobly bearing the bloody burden; and that he who does not this, makes not the return due for the civil blessings he enjoys, and is, so far, not a faithful and loyal citizen. The minister of God, in such a crisis, has his allotted sphere and proper part to perform. He can not, without incurring grave responsibilities, in his public teaching or private example, ignore the fact of the war, and of the duties and dangers growing out of it. Even if he should believe his country to be in the wrong, it is very questionable, when the die is once cast; a vast and overwhelming majority having decided whether he has the right to hold out in such a course of indifference and opposition, so weakening, as far as his example goes, our cause at home, and in effect, to that extent, giving aid and comfort to the enemy. For if majorities, however controlling, are thus virtually denied the right of governing and shaping the destinies of their country, all the compromises of society are overthrown, a spirit of faction is encouraged, and a blow, fatal in its character, struck at the unity and moral strength of the state. If, under such circumstances, a man will hold out, when the struggle for very existence as a nation is going on, the alternative is left him, and he ought to embrace it, of renouncing his allegiance, and going where he thinks the *right* prevails. But apart from natural instincts, or the love of country, which the Scriptures recognize and encourage, we have the sanction of God himself, as he called his people of old to wage war against their enemies round about them, showing that war is not of necessity an evil *per se;* that the invader may be righteously driven out, and that God's ministers, like his prophets of old, as they were directed by him, may, in their allotted sphere, instruct and animate the people in their duties, at a time, as *now*, which involves the interests of religion, not less than independence, liberty, and life. As to the "judgment of charity," which Mr. G. affirms should prevent us from calling our enemies an infidel host, or vandals, and cause us to esteem them as not more infidel or irreligious than ourselves, though we are, indeed, sinners against God, have much infidelity among us, and have come

grievously short of our duty, as individuals and a people—
and while *charity* as to the individual is worthy of the high
encomium passed upon it by the Apostle—we have yet to
learn that, as to a people, charity calls upon us to shut our
eyes to some of the most patent facts of history, as when we
speak of a corrupt branch of the Church of Christ, and the
states under its sway; or of the French in the days of their
bloody revolution, as a nation of infidels; of the Mormons
now, as an adulterous and profligate sect; or as to the masses
of the free States of America, and especially those of New-
England, as being, what some of their own most enlightened
writers declare them to be, strongly infidel. *Where*, we ask—
these writers not less than ourselves being the judges—is the
hotbed of infidelity on this continent? From whence have
the numberless isms of the day, almost without an exception,
proceeded? Where has the spirit of agrarianism shown itself
most rampant? Where has the doctrine of "higher law"
been proclaimed with unblushing front, and openly advocated?
the present Federal Secretary of State—the master spirit, perhaps, of this crusade against the South and against slavery—
being the higher-law apostle; a *crusade* based upon the
avowed declaration, that, if the Scriptures sanction slavery,
they are not to be heeded. And, where on the other hand,
have Unitarianism, Universalism, transcendentalism, Mormon-
ism, spiritualism, and higher-lawism, had the least hold, and made
the smallest progress, but in those States where the institution
of domestic slavery has prevailed with its conservative tendencies, and *where*, also, the originally predominating elements
of population have continued to exercise a happy sway?
While all this is said in no spirit of boasting, nor the fact denied that in the North are *many, very many* conservative and
pious people, and that the Protestant Episcopal Church there,
for example, has made remarkable progress—being the main
bulwark, as Mr. G. himself has hitherto been accustomed to
affirm, against the infidelity around it—it is yet most apparent that infidelity has fearful sway — that abolitionism is
but one of its multiform phases—and that, in this war, which
abolitionism had much to do in forcing upon the country, and
is now recklessly urging on, we may, without doing violence

to the judgment of charity, speak of an infidel host, and of *vandals*, too. For *what* has the war been in the Border States, in our captured cities, wherever, in short, the enemy has penetrated, but one series of shocking vandalism? 'Calling our slaves to insurrection, arming them against us, destroying the property of unoffending citizens, defacing our churches, brutally treating our women and children, and now developing itself more plainly than ever in the monstrous order of General Pope. Was it a breach of charity to speak of the ancient Goths and Vandals, as such? or for the persecuted and flying Huguenots to call their merciless enemies infidels and murderers? and is charity, the very bond of peace and of all virtues, to be held up to us now as a shield and cloak to our foes? We do not mean that all of those who are warring against us are infidels or vandals; God forbid! Already many illustrious exceptions have appeared, and we know that thousands are deceived and misled. But in speaking as we do, it is of the mass, of the spirit animating them, and of their plainly marked conduct in the prosecution of the war. It is *passing strange* that a minister of God, in so speaking, though he may consistently therewith pray for our enemies, as I trust every good man does, should yet therein violate his "ordination vows," to maintain and set forward, as much as lieth in him, quietness, peace, and love among all Christian people, and especially among those that are, or shall be, committed to his charge—and this in a Southern community, a part of a ravaged land, and when there should be but one sentiment prevailing. The most effective and only way, indeed, of setting forward peace and quietness between the Southern and Northern people, is to drive out the invaders, and bring the war to a close. *Are arms* not to be taken up by the members of the Church against a ruthless foe? Are the dearest rights of men not to be protected? And are *we forbidden* to speak of the spirit, conduct, and acts of our enemies as they deserve? Is all this incompatible with a general spirit of charity? Do we not pray that our own soldiers may be saved from all undue excess in the hour of victory, from the temptations to which they may be exposed, and that peace may be restored?

On the other hand—and I speak in all kindness—may not a

minister sadly fail to set forward "quietness, peace, and love" among the people committed to his charge, by persistently declining to say Amen to a prayer put forth by his Bishop and read before the congregation, when his opinion as to a *fact declarative* made in the prayer is well known, so that he would in doing otherwise compromise no opinion or violate his conscience, simply giving his assent to the petitions therein, as he reads them himself, and as would be understood by any one present? Is not such a course, under the circumstances, unprecedented in the Church of Christ? A minister kneeling at the same altar with his Bishop, and refusing to respond to the petitions he offers up, though they may be accompanied by a declaration to which he can not assent, and is so understood not to assent? Does it not encourage those of the people who sympathize with him to persist in a like course? Does it not wound the feelings of others, sadly mar the devotional feelings of the congregation, and strike a well-nigh fatal blow at the spirit of prayer itself, without which there can be no quietness, peace, and love? And rather than persist in such a course, with such consequences inevitably resulting, if indeed his conscience will not allow him to do otherwise, do not his ordination vows call upon him to weigh well a position fraught with such unhappy consequences for the Church of Christ? It is with exceeding pain that I contemplate the circumstances which make the utterance of such convictions proper on this occasion. It would rejoice me to see my brethren, who, I think, have greatly erred in this matter, pursuing a course not to the violation of their consciences, for that I think by no means necessary, *but a course* which would give unity to prayer at least, and deliver them from an attitude of separation in the devotions of God's people.

As to the eighth proposition, to which Mr. G. can not assent, "that our last Diocesan Council has not exceeded the usual custom of the Church in political legislation, and that there has been no teaching of the clergy beyond what was meet, considering the exigencies of the times in relation to war and its adjuncts," it is only necessary to remark that there was, at the meeting referred to, no "political legislation" which could have been beyond its province, but simply a declaration, by report and resolutions, of the feelings and opinions of the Convention as to the grave questions that have agitated Church and State, including a very decided expression as to the present *war*. That this exceeded the *usual custom* of the American Church can not be said, for there has been no custom of the sort, the present revolution being altogether new and unparalleled. At the breaking out of the old Revolution, the Church was in an organized state in but few of the colonies, these forming a part of the Establishment, and in two of which, Maryland and Virginia, where the number was greatest, at least two thirds of the clergy were loyalists, the remaining portion being true to the cause of liberty, and casting all their influence in its behalf, a few going so far as to take up arms. There was no Bishop, as now, nor Conventions organized, as we have them. When the yoke was thrown off, the Church in America was considered separate from that in England. Our condition now being peculiar and unprecedented, the action taken by our Convention was likewise new, except as to that in other confederate dioceses previously, and was becoming the *occasion*. From the time of Constantine, when the empire became nominally Christian, down to the present, throughout the history of the Church of England, nothing can be found to indicate that our recent action was inconsistent with the practice of the Church, though in a sense unusual and extraordinary. As to the teaching of the clergy on the subject of the war and its adjuncts, if there has been any error, it has been in not coming up to the spiritual demands of such a crisis, rather than in exceeding the bounds of propriety. I should blush for the Church and mourn over her indifference and timidity, if nothing more, if she had failed to give that vast moral influence which she possesses to the *righteous claims* of the State with which at such a time, as always, her interests and welfare are closely and indissolubly connected.

As to the ninth proposition, to which Mr. G. can not assent, "that any man has the right to go behind the words of prayer, and judge another as to whether he prays *ex animo*," I ask, Who has so affirmed, who *maintains it?* In reply to a remark made in the conversation first herein referred to, I did say, and still hold, that the use of the other part of the prayer, though omitting the declaratory words "which has been forced upon us," ought to be sufficiently decisive of the opinions and sympathies of a clergyman so using it, as to the present conflict. I did say, and still hold as a general proposition, without judging any man, that it would not of *necessity* be *so decisive*. That one, for example, may repeat the prayer as here affirmed, *ex animo*, if you choose, and *yet* not in the sense that *another does*, and that when such an one prays for victory, and that the Confederacy may flourish and prosper, the point is not whether he prays with a general spirit of devout submission to the will of God—for this all good people are supposed to do—*but what* does he *wish to be God's will* in the matter. He may simply pray that if God wills, let it be so, while there is not, in fact, an actual desire on his part which is lawful that God would will it to be so. As in the case of our Saviour, who prayed, "Let this cup pass from me," manifestly wishing in his human nature that it might be God's will to permit it, but straightway adding, "Nevertheless, not *my will* but *thine* be done." It is well known that certain of our prayers in the Church, as in the Baptismal Office, are repeated by persons who differ doctrinally in a different sense; and why may it not be so as to the prayer before us?

As to the tenth proposition, to which Mr. G. can not assent, "That the special prayer now in use in this Diocese is based upon the words, 'which has been forced upon us,' and without these becomes in effect no prayer for the times," I am not aware that any such statement has been made. It may have been remarked, indeed, that in one sense *it is*, or *has been* made, the key to the prayer, or something like this. But taken without the words referred to, those who have been most decided in the expression of opinion, on the subject, have, I believe, admitted that the prayer would yet be suitable and comprehensive, and cover the ground generally which such a prayer should do. It is strange that the words, "which has been forced upon us," as spoken of the war, should be regarded by any in the light of "gratuitous information to the Almighty." For what can be said in prayer, of a declarative kind, which is not familiar to God? He knoweth what we have need of before we ask him. The question, in such cases, ought to be, Is *the statement* or declaration made, in itself, or its connections, proper and becoming? As *here*, the words, " which has been forced upon us," naturally occur in proceeding to a petition touching the war, and are as proper as the words, " Thy injured people," which precede them ; for we are not an *injured people* as to *that* at least, if the war has not been forced upon us. Why the one is so much objected to, and not the other, I am at a loss to imagine. *Wherein*, as to *that*, have we been wronged, if we are equally as, or more responsible than our enemies in bringing on the war, unless it be in their conduct in its prosecution? As to which, it must be remarked that the prayer was put forth, and the words, " Thy injured people," acquiesced in, before the war had assumed its present aspect, and when the injury could only have been referred to the manner of its inception. The words so much objected to have a precedent as to their being declaratory, in the universal practice of man in prayer. The prayers of the Church, as they constitute a fixed part of the Liturgy, are of necessity *general*, even the special prayers and thanksgivings in the Prayer-Book partaking of the generality. A prayer, on the other hand, put forth by a Bishop for extraordinary occasions, may naturally be expected to go more into detail, and would not be marred of necessity by a *declaration* like that in question.

I *have said* that if the matter had been suggested to me at the time of composing the prayer, the *words* might have been omitted, simply on the ground of such a statement of fact being unusual in the Liturgy of the Church, though never expressing regret that it had been done. After further reflection, however, and a deliberate survey of the whole subject, I am not prepared to repeat the remark. As before remarked, the words came in naturally in the connection where they occur. No special thought was given to them, nor did it occur to me that any one's conscience would be officially burdened thereby.

In regard to the remark made by Mr. Gillette, that the action of his brethren " partakes largely of an intolerant, sectarian, and persecuting spirit, a spirit which says you must think and speak as I do, or not at all," I am persuaded he is sadly in error. He must not forget that the plea of persecution has often been made, though never so sincerely, by those who naturally sought some shelter from the troubles which their own errors had brought upon them. Where is the evidence of intolerance, of sectarianism, of persecution? If he had the *right* to hold and act upon a political opinion, as he maintains, and that not only privately, as an individual, but in his official character in the Church, declaring therein, as publicly as any one could do in conversation, "that the war has not been forced upon us," so expressing, as it were, the voice of a parish, or of the rector thereof, at least, and making an issue on a prayer put forth by authority, had not the Convention also the right to make an opposite declaration, in the behalf of the other parishes represented, and of the Church at large? It would be monstrous, were it otherwise. Individual ministers might, in that case, do the Church an *incalculable injury*, and yet the Church, forsooth, be stopped from a word in its own vindication!

But, beyond this, what have the clergy, as a body, done? Mr. Gillette appears to regard the action of the Convention as having been taken chiefly for the purpose of condemning himself and Mr. Brown, whereas, other and much more important purposes were before it, animating it in its course, and shaping its actions. If, in the result of the elections, Mr. Gillette finds evidence of intolerance and persecution, he is not, perhaps, aware of the pain with which that result was looked to, by some, if not all of his brethren, though felt to be necessary. He may not be aware, again, that the object was *not* to wound or injure him, but to do justice to the Church, an issue having been made, first of all, by himself. The Convention, feeling that, under all the circumstances, to continue him in the position he had hitherto held, as one of the oldest and most prominent Presbyters of the Diocese, would have been to sanction his course in the matters herein referred to, besides being in the teeth of its own solemn declaration as to the war in the Confederacy, and our relations to the Church in the United States, and action thereon. For the spirit which animated the Convention, in all its proceedings, the members doubtless felt that they would be responsible to God, and, I trust, may be able to give a good account.

To one part I should bear testimony, that, throughout the meeting of Convention, I remember not to have heard a word of personal unkindness toward Mr. Gillette uttered, nor did I see any thing in the conduct of the members incompatible with Christian charity for him. I trust he may sooner or later discover that they have not acted as he has charged.

And, finally, as to what Mr. Gillette remarks, "that he feels his brethren are proposing a new test of fitness for ministerial labor among them, hitherto unknown in the Church, saying, You must believe with us politically, or you can not labor in the Church with us; we cannot fraternize with you, without this; but we will, by our acts, publicly say, You are unworthy to labor with us as a minister in the Church of God," I can only say, that he sadly errs in his conclusions from what transpired; that his brethren have set up no new test, as will appear from what has already been said; and that, so far as their action in Convention bears on the subject of his remark, it has been simply to the effect, not that he is unworthy to labor with them, but that his course, of late, in the Diocese, has been inimical to the dearest interests of the States, has seriously affected his usefulness in the Church, and, as far as such an example can, at the present time, will affect the welfare of the Church itself. For these consequences, surely, they are not responsible. It is a time which tries men's souls, and for his conduct every one will have to bear his own burden.

In reply to the Bishop's strictures on the ten propositions, to which I can not assent, and only one of which, the eighth, he thinks had foundation in truth, I would state, that I addressed a letter to Rev. Mr. Wagner, asking whether he did not, in effect, assert some of the propositions named. Rev. Mr. Brown made a minute of the conversation at the time, and this minute has since fallen into my hands. I have compared the Bishop's statements, Mr. Wagner's letter, and Mr. Brown's minutes, and for convenience of reference, place them side by side.

The Bishop.

"As to the first proposition, to which Mr. Gillette can not assent, 'that a Christian minister has no right to be guided by his own conscientious convictions of duty, although those convictions may be contrary to the convictions of many or all of his brethren, I do not understand it to have been made directly or indirectly."

"As to the second proposition to which Mr. Gillette cannot assent, 'that a minister of the Gospel violates the peace of the Church, when, in his own sphere, he conscientiously performs what he believes to be his duty, in accordance to the ritual of the Church, and with the permission and sanction of his Bishop, and without transgressing any law or regulation of the Church,' I do not understand that in this form any such proposition has been made."

"As to the third proposition, 'that a Bishop has no right to grant permission, to one or a number of his clergy, to omit a sentence, or a part of a sentence, in a special prayer put forth by himself for extraordinary occasions,' I am not aware that it has been maintained."

"As to the fourth proposition, that a minister is responsible for the political sentiments of his congregation, and if he can not guide and control them in politics, he had better leave them to the care of some one else, I can only express my surprise that Mr. Gillette should understand any one to have made it, and add, emphatically, God forbid that it should be so."

"As to the fifth proposition, 'that the Council of the Church in solemn conclave, is bound to listen to the voice of the outside world, and publicly censure a brother clergyman for what they deem a political heresy, passing a series of resolutions, and requiring them to be read in open church, thereby intending him to define his position politically,' it certainly has not been done to my knowledge."

Rev. Mr. Wagner.

"A minister has *no right* to stand out against the expressed opinion of his Bishop and brethren of the clergy, in matters which do not involve the faith. But he is bound to yield his convictions, to their advice, and *act in concert with them* for the general good and order, *or else to go out from them into some congenial field*, in which opportunity is afforded for the free exercise of his convictions; and no permission of the Bishop could affect my view of this obligation so to act."

"I consider that Mr. Brown and yourself are chargeable for having *violated the harmony* (not the peace) of the Church's operations, by your general course of conduct in reference to the performance of public services, and by your lack of interest in the political crisis which has convulsed the country — even though the Bishop granted the permission, under the circumstances."

"I think the Bishop had no right to grant the permission to one or more of his clergy to omit a portion of a prayer which he had canonically put forth, for the general use of the *whole* Church, and I so expressed myself."

"If a rector can not influence his congregation so as to promote unity in them, *unity of sentiment with the whole Church in a crisis such as this*, it is evidence of his insufficiency for such a charge, and he ought to relinquish it."

"I believe that the future prosperity of the Church in this State demanded that the recent Convention should express its decided disapproval of the reported course which had been pursued by yourself, Mr. Brown, and some of the laity, during the year previous, and it was under this pressure that your names were removed from the various Committees, etc.

"It was to meet this demand that a portion of the Bishop's Address was referred to a Special Committee, that a distinct utterance of our sympathy with our country's cause might be given by the Convention, and the report, preamble, and resolutions adopted.

"I believed, (and so must you have believed, when you read it

Rev. Mr. Brown.

"Rev. Mr. Wagner asserted that Rev. Messrs. Gillette and Brown violated the *peace* and *harmony* of the Church."

Again, "were violating the *peace* and *harmony* of the Church in refusing to pray that prayer as set forth by the Bishop."

"Rev. C. Gillette said the maker of the prayer had the power to authorize an omission therefrom, if he chose, and he had so chosen. Rev. Mr. Wagner denied the right to do this."

"The Rev. Mr. Wagner said that the omission of Rev. C. Gillette's name from all committees of the Convention, was designed as a special rebuke to him. That the report and resolutions of the Committee on that part of the Bishop's Address, having reference to the relation of the Church in this Diocese, to the Confederate States, and to the Protestant Episcopal Church in the United States, had been freely canvassed by the majority of the members, before they were presented to the Convention. That they were understood by this majority, and on their adoption by the whole Convention, to have been drawn up for the purpose of testing the political standing of the Rev. C. Gillette. That it

The Bishop.

"As to the sixth proposition to which Mr. Gillette can not assent, 'that the present war is one for the sake of piety, and that the very existence of morality, virtue, and religion in the South is involved in its issue,' I am not aware that it has been made.".

Rev. Mr. Wagner.

in connection with the other action,) that the resolution requiring 'it to be read before all the congregations,' was designed to effect the following results: that the sentiments expressed by the Bishop, and indorsed by the Convention in terms so strong, might be made available to the instruction of every member of the Church, in every congregation; that the clergy might be aided in building up their people in the sentiments which their brethren (clerical and lay) throughout the entire South, had uttered with singular unanimity, and that those of the clergy, whose course had made them obnoxious to the course of the community at large, might be compelled to publish, with their own lips, that the position they occupied was in antagonism with the voice of the Church in the Confederate States, and more especially with the Church in the Diocese of Texas.

"I *did not say* that it was talked of among a majority of the members of the Convention before the Committee made their report; though *I did say your conduct* had been spoken of very freely by members of the Convention, not only during but before and after its session."

Rev. Mr. Brown.

was believed by several, if not every member of the Convention, that the Rev. C. Gillette would refuse to read the report, and the passages pointed out in said report. In answer, or by way of comment, Rev. C. Gillette said that it was very evident to his mind that his clerical brethren had resolved themselves into a political clique, to determine his political position."

"The Bishop and Mr. Wagner both insisted that the war was not a political war, but one involving the very being of religion and of the Church."

The Bishop himself has at various times, and on several occasions, used the following language, which seemed to me to amount to my proposition: "At a time, as *now*, which involves the interests of religion, not less than independence, liberty, and life." Speaking of the confederate successes near Richmond in 1862, he says: "It may not unfrequently be concluded, with humble confidence, that God is on the side of those in their successes, who are struggling against a powerful, malignant, and exterminating foe, for national independence, for religion, liberty, and right." "Are we not struggling for our *very existence* as a people, for religion, and liberty?" "In the yoke which subjugation by our foes would impose, and the bloody horrors, ever attending the efforts to throw it off, that our very religion, as we now have it and enjoy it, would be lamentably involved, passing under a dark cloud; all ecclesiastical organizations, as now existing, being broken up, and a scattered and almost exterminated people, as we would be, forced to worship the God of our fathers in secret places, in the wilderness, in mountains and caves of the earth. In this sense, and to this extent, we are fighting for religion." From the Bishop's own language, I do not see what reason he has to quarrel with my proposition.

The Bishop.	*Mr. Wagner.*	*Mr. Brown.*
"As to the tenth proposition, 'That the special prayer now in use in this diocese is based upon the words "which has been forced upon us," and without these becomes in effect no prayer for the times,' I am not aware that any such statement has been made."	"I asserted that the whole basis of the prayer was found in that circumstance," (expressed in the words "which has been forced upon us,") "and without the acceptation of that clause, would become, in my mind, an unsuitable prayer for the times."	"Mr. Wagner insisted that the prayer was based upon the words omitted, and when these were removed, the prayer was all but valueless. To this the Bishop was understood to assent."

From the preceding statements, I think it is very evident that the understanding, and the recollection of Messrs. Wagner and Brown, sustain me very fully in regard to the sense of the propositions. As one is partially granted by the Bishop, there remain but two, the seventh and ninth, which are not already established. That these propositions, when put in writing, assume a new form, and one of much greater importance than when merely talked over and loosely asserted, I can well understand. But how the Bishop should have understood so differently from all the rest who took part in that conversation, or how, in the few days which elapsed between the conversation and the writing of his answer to my propositions, these points should have passed from his mind, is more difficult to comprehend. The whole answer looks to me like special pleading, and the spirit of the reply is any thing but what I could have wished. It seems to me that the Bishop has determined, having, as he thinks, the power, by his office and influence, to put me down and drive me from the Diocese, my offense being that I am not sufficiently committed to the cause of the South.

How far it becomes necessary for me to answer the Bishop in his statements, or implications, impugning my actions or motives, there may be room to doubt; and yet something is due to myself in this connection. I do not propose to do more than refer to some of the more important points laid down by the Bishop in his communication, as referring to myself individually, or to the great principles affecting religion and the Church.

In the beginning, the Bishop says: "Unhappy results have already transpired, but not, I am persuaded, through the fault or error of their brethren, as to Rev. Messrs. Gillette and Brown. May not the present state of things, as to *them*, be attributable rather to erroneous opinion and position in the outset, and misconception, in consequence, as to what has since occurred?"

Let us examine for a moment this "erroneous opinion and position," and the "unhappy results." The erroneous opinion consisted in this, that they did not believe the war forced upon the South by the North. How shall they be convicted of error in holding this opinion? Is the Bishop, or are the clergy in the Diocese of Texas competent to decide them in error in this matter? Does such a decision come within their province in council assembled, even if they were competent in point of ability? Has this matter been so decided that the Bishop can now certainly and infallibly declare one or more of his clergy in error in opinion, because they assert that they do not believe the North forced this war upon the South? Is it not possible that the opinion as above stated is true, and that those who hold the opposite are in error? So much for the erroneous *opinion*. Now, what was the erroneous *position* held by the Rev. Messrs. Gillette and Brown? I know of no erroneous position for which they could be held justly responsible. With the Bishop's permission to omit, they did not assert in the special prayer that the war was forced upon the South by the North. If this was an error, could it be charged on them? They used a permission granted by the Bishop; if it placed them in an erroneous position, why did the Bishop lead them into it by giving his permission? In consequence of this permission being used, the Bishop forbade Rev. Messrs. Gillette and Brown from officiating, on any occasion, outside of the cure of St. David's. In this prohibition, the Bishop plainly exceeded his authority. Mr. Brown being a deacon, the Bishop could direct where he should officiate; the Rev. Mr. Gillette being a presbyter, the Bishop could exercise no such authority. But to waive the question of authority, if their position in not officiating outside of St. David's parish was one of error, who placed them in it? Upon whom rested the responsibility?

What are the unhappy results referred to? Evidently discord among brethren, and a forbidding to preach the Gospel where it is needed. Who is to blame for this? Was there any good ground for brethren to be offended because the Rev. Messrs. Gillette and Brown did not agree in an opinion expressed by their Bishop—an opinion which any one had a right to entertain or not, as he pleased? When rightly considered, what possible ground was there for offense in this? Who was to blame that the Gospel was not preached? The Bishop gave leave to omit certain words in a prayer, and then forbids the clergymen to officiate outside of a single cure, even if traveling and desired to officiate, because they do just what he gave them leave to do. Who is to blame for these "unhappy results"?

In speaking of the first proposition, the Bishop says: "Has a clergyman, or any man, a right to be guided by conscientious convictions, unless he has taken the pains to enlighten his conscience, by a well-informed judgment? Suppose, as in the case before us, these convictions are based upon a political opinion, the party entertaining them, all the while eschewing politics—has he not reason to distrust himself?" The assumption, that I have "taken no pains to enlighten my conscience by a well-informed judgment," is wholly gratuitous. I do not claim to have ever taken an active part in politics. But I do claim to have noticed passing events, and to have read newspapers enough to form an opinion upon the great political questions of the day; and I do not think the language used by the Bishop either proper or justifiable in the present case.

Again the Bishop says: "Would not common prudence dictate that he should be willing to take the opinion of the statesmen of the country, if you please, the wisest laymen of the Church, just as he would expect a politician or a man of the world, in matters of religious faith and practice, to take counsel of the divines of the Church?"

What does all this mean? Are the wisest laymen of the

Church all holding one opinion in the matters here spoken of? If there is a divided sentiment, what shall determine which party is right? Shall we follow the greatest number? If so, the Bishop himself is wrong, for those who maintain his opinion are largely in the minority. Shall the ablest men decide it? Who shall point them out? I think they are *here* and everywhere opposed to the Bishop.

But does the Bishop mean that the politician, or "the man of the world," when he takes counsel of the divines of the Church, on matters where there is dispute, follows their counsels without using his own judgment? If that is what he means, is the implied assertion true? Do politicians or men of the world do this? Again I ask, What does all this mean? Is it for talk? or to blind? or what is its object?

What the Bishop further says under the first proposition, if it means any thing, means that a man who conscientiously believes he is right, must even give up the holding of an opinion, or go out of the country, because a majority of his neighbors do not think as he does—reasoning which, if it were true, would once have driven the Saviour of men out of the world, and would now drive all faithful ministers out of it also. "Under such unhappy circumstances, is he to remain where he is?" The Bishop here intimates his desire for me to leave his diocese, but I trust will not insist, unless I shall find it convenient.

Under the second proposition, the Bishop says: "A minister *may so far err* in the *manner* of performing what he conceives to be his duty, as to violate the peace of the Church, though in letter he may not seem to violate the Church's ritual or laws." What the Bishop here means by his italicized "*manner*," I have not the slightest idea. He evidently has found something very objectionable in my "manner" of performing service, but what, I have no means of divining. I would not refer to it, except to show how fault-finding are the times.

Under the fourth proposition, the Bishop accuses me of criminal silence upon "special topics, which the time demands for the improvement of a people; *as for example*, the temptation of extortion, of revenge, of profanity, of reliance upon an arm of flesh, and undue absorption—in short, in the things of the present, in its extraordinary character, to the neglect of spiritual things." I can simply say that, in my judgment, this accusation is without just foundation. I do not claim to have treated these subjects as the Bishop has. But that I have been silent upon them, I do not conceive to be a fair statement; that I have not been sufficiently enthusiastic in the cause of the Southern Confederacy to suit the Bishop, is quite evident, and that it is a very grievous offense, in his judgment, is also evident from all he says. Another complaint the Bishop makes under this head is as follows : "He may show a decidedly partisan spirit by allowing himself, for whatever reason, to cherish most, if not all, his private sympathetic associations with a certain class of his congregation, and these generally supposed to be disaffected toward the Government, or at least not sympathizing with the country in its struggle."

The associations here complained of, were with intimate friends, some of them of twenty years' standing. The Bishop had known these persons a much shorter time, and much less intimately than I had done. He chose to break away from them, although strong supporters of the Church, and some of them communicants, because he thought they were not sufficiently warm in the Southern cause, and actually ceased to visit them. He desired me to follow his example, and because I could not see and act in this matter as he did, it made an occasion for a grave charge. According to him, a man must abandon his long-cherished friends, if they do not go strong for the Southern Confederacy.

In my use of the word "conclave," in the fifth proposition, I had no reference of course to an assembly of Rome's cardinals. I rather used it in a much more common signification, to mean a meeting for Church legislation. Even the Bishop himself could not have supposed that I used it to signify a secret assembly of cardinals.

Of the action of this meeting, he says : "It was most proper and becoming that the Convention should solemnly declare 'that this unnatural war was forced upon us,' for the vindication of the Bishop, of a suffering country, of the Church's integrity, its members of all degrees having embarked their

4

lives and fortunes in the struggle, and for its justification before God in praying for victory over our foes."

From this language of the Bishop concerning the *propriety* of the action of the Convention, I must certainly dissent; and it would not surprise me if the time should yet come when the Bishop himself will dissent from it also. His whole reasoning here, strikes me as untenable, and that which will not bear the scrutiny of sober thought when the excitement of the present times shall have passed away.

In commenting on the sixth proposition, the Bishop uses this language: "Our very religion, as we now have it and enjoy it, would be lamentably involved, passing under a dark cloud, all ecclesiastical organizations as now existing being broken up, and a scattered and almost exterminated people, as we would be, forced to worship the God of our fathers in secret places, in the wilderness, in mountains and in caves of the earth. In this sense, and to this extent, we are fighting for religion, and rely upon God for deliverance." If the Bishop does not say to all intents and purposes in the above, "that the present war is one for the sake of piety, and that the very existence of morality, virtue, and religion in the South are involved in its issue," then what does he say? and what does he mean? Under the seventh proposition, the Bishop asks: "What clergyman of the Church has harangued his people or endeavored, etc., to arouse in them a spirit of war?" Could the Bishop ask this question publicly and men be free to answer, there are not a few men who would say to him in response: "Thou art the man!" "I understand that the injunction of our Saviour imposes the duty of allegiance to the government under which we live, and of supporting it in defense of its liberties, and that this allegiance or fidelity to the state—a natural obligation as society is formed, not less than the subject of divine injunction—is wholly incompatible with the desire, or willingness, or even indifference, that a government at war with our own and seeking to overthrow it, should succeed in the attempt and be reëstablished in its stead."

The Bishop could not have stopped to think how much such reasoning made against himself, and all who went into secession; breaking up the lawful government, to which they owed allegiance, and attempting to establish another government on its ruins and in its stead. Surely, if the Bishop's reasoning be true, this was all wrong, and I was right in doing nothing to overthrow and destroy my government.

Again the Bishop says of a minister, "if he should believe his country to be in the wrong, it is very questionable, when the die is once cast, a vast and overwhelming majority having decided, whether he has the right to hold out in such a course of indifference and opposition, so weakening, as far as his example goes, our cause at home, and, in effect, to that extent giving aid and comfort to the enemy. For if majorities, however controlling, are thus virtually denied the right of governing and shaping the destinies of their country, all the compromises of society are overthrown, a spirit of faction is encouraged, and a blow, fatal in its character, struck at the unity and moral strength of the state."

How the Bishop could have penned such language under the circumstances, and not have felt that he was strongly condemning himself and his coadjutors, is hard to understand. The rebellion had been commenced by a minority in the seceding States, and gained a majority only when the people, disarmed and through fear, were made to engage in a struggle which they at first loathed and shuddered to commence. But suppose that every individual human being in the seceded States had gone willingly into this matter of tearing up and dismembering the government, still they would have been largely in the minority, when considered in relation to the whole government, to which the Bishop, and I, and all owed our allegiance; and, according to his own argument, even if he thought the Government wrong, he had no right to oppose, or to set himself in opposition to it. I do not myself subscribe to the doctrine of "My country, right or wrong," or that I am to go with the majority, even if I may think it wrong. For my Bible tells me: "It is better to go alone to do well, than with a multitude to do evil." I could have wished the Bishop to have stopped short of trying to make me guilty of treason by "giving aid and comfort to the enemy," not that I fear its consequences, but the spirit manifested does not look "lovely and of good report."

Again, the Bishop says: "As He (God) called his people of old to wage war against their enemies, showing that war is not of necessity an evil *per se;* that the invader may be righteously driven out, and that God's ministers, like his prophets of old, as they were directed by him, may, in their allotted sphere, instruct and animate the people in their duties, at a time as *now*, which involves the interests of religion, not less than independence, liberty, and life." In order to make this reasoning good, I think the following assumptions must first be proved, namely, that the people of the South are, *par excellence*, the people of God, and the people of the North heathens or infidels. That we have a government *established* separate and distinct from that of the North, making us a foreign nation owing no allegiance to the Government of the United States. That our ministers in this respect occupy the place of God's prophets of old, and are inspired or directly commanded of God to incite the people to war.

The Bishop says again: "Is not such a course unprecedented in the Church of Christ? A minister kneeling at the same altar with his Bishop, and refusing to respond to the petitions he offers up, though they may be accompanied by a declaration to which he can not assent." I might answer, truly: "Is not such a course unprecedented in the Church of Christ? a Bishop insisting upon the introduction of a declaration into a prayer, expressive of an opinion of his, but disbelieved by many—insisting that men should say Amen to it, whether they believe it or not—thus striking a well-nigh fatal blow at the spirit of prayer itself?" I might add much more of the same sort, as the Bishop has done, and with any right-minded man, it would all apply to the Bishop and not to me. Through all his reasoning, the Bishop seems to forget that this whole matter commenced, and is prosecuted by his trenching on the sacred rights of others, in attempting to compel them to believe and do that which he has no right to attempt; that he considers himself and others greatly aggrieved because he can not have his own way in manufacturing public opinion, and making all men assent to what he proclaims. He seems to forget that a portion of the community have any right left them—even the right to an opinion, quietly held. According to his idea, the greatest thing and the greatest good is the Southern Confederacy—any thing which militates against that is an evil, and must be opposed—every man that does not give his hearty support to this, must be silenced, or driven out of the country. Even in the Church, there can be no prayer or worship equal to that which prays for the Southern Confederacy, or justifies the rebellion, by proclaiming that those who fight her battles are acting on the defensive. This is not only evidently the Bishop's view of the subject, as appears from his writings; but he absolutely forbids service and the preaching of the Gospel, unless the minister first declare that the war "has been forced upon us."

In his argument, the Bishop evidently assumes that all the morality, and religion, and high-toned honorable feeling, and every principle of right are with the South, while all evil, and wickedness, and aggression, and irreligion are with the North. According to his views, there may be, and are, some good people in the North; but the masses, and those who engage in the war, are infidels and vandals. The Bishop may change his mind before he dies, provided his nice talk of living in mountain caves should be thought better of, as no doubt it will, when he becomes better acquainted with the Northern people.

How far the Bishop's reasoning, in regard to the eighth proposition, is correct, the action of the Convention will show, and men who read it must decide for themselves. His reference to the state of the Church in the "old Revolution," if properly applied, would have led the Church to have been quiet and minded her own business until the war was over and the boundaries of territory settled, so that if it was necessary to form a new organization, we might know what States belonged to the Confederate States. Our dioceses were organized, and our bishops in charge, and no further organization for the good of the Church was required. The only thing to be gained by further organization was to add strength to the rebellion, by giving moral power to the Government.

The Bishop claims that the Church did not exceed her custom, because hitherto she had no custom. Is this so? Has not her custom been to be silent, and not to legislate on matters of state? I am speaking of our own branch of the Church in this country. When he refers to the Church from Constantine down, he speaks of it when the Church is connected with the state, and of course it does not apply to our present reasoning.

In regard to the ninth proposition, and praying *ex animo*, I thought at the time of the conversation, and I still think that the Bishop desired to draw from me an expression as to whether I prayed, "That if it be God's will, let it be so," or whether I had an "actual desire that God would will it to be so." That he insisted that I should use the prayer in the latter sense, and it was in this connection that I thought the Bishop exceeding his province in wishing me to pray that "God would will it to be so," rather than "to let it be so if it was his will." I did not think that he or any man was able to take such a supervision over any other. It was in this connection that he desired so earnestly to know what I wished in regard to the final result of the war, as referred to by Mr. Brown.

Under the tenth proposition, the Bishop asks: Where is the evidence of intolerance, of sectarianism, of persecution?

The evidence of intolerance is found in the fact that my brethren of the clergy would not ask Mr. Brown or myself to officiate for them or assist them when we were in their parishes. That they would not officiate for us, or assist in the service, when visiting in our parish. It is true, I did not visit the parish of any of my brethren so as to be asked to officiate, but Mr. Brown spent several weeks in the parish of a brother, who did not extend the courtesy of asking him to assist in the service or preach, giving as a reason, that Mr. Brown omitted the words of the prayer heretofore referred to. Those of the clergy who came to our parish refused (with one exception) to take part in the service or preach, and that exception subsequently refused, while staying at the house of the Bishop. This intolerance is essentially sectarian. Again, the proof of intolerance is found in the action of the Convention, which studiously dropped our names from all committees, by way of reproof for our supposed offense. It is found in the act of the Bishop himself, in forbidding Mr. Brown and myself to officiate outside of the cure of St. David's; when Mr. Brown had been ordained deacon, with the express understanding, on the part of the Bishop, that he should perform missionary duty in places contiguous to Austin, while he further pursued his studies under my direction. All these acts are intolerance in the worst form. They are sectarian in character, and in spirit as well as deed, persecution.

I might add much more in connection with this communication of the Bishop, but I have probably said enough to show its spirit and point out some of its inconsistencies.

The following, in regard to Mr. Brown's officiating, will explain itself:

"MY DEAR BISHOP: Could you not make an arrangement for Mr. Brown to hold service at two or three places, within twenty or thirty miles of this, so that he might do missionary duty? If you think such an arrangement well, I would suggest the neighborhood of Mr. Williams's and San Marcos, where Mr. Yellowly and his family expect to be after the first of next year, and they are very desirous of having the services of the Church.

"If such an arrangement could be made, Mr. Brown could be doing something for the Church while he is pursuing his studies. Yours truly, CHARLES GILLETTE.
"AUSTIN, December 2, 1862."

"DEAR BROTHER GILLETTE: I am much engaged at this moment, and will converse with you, in reference to the subject of your note, to-morrow afternoon, D. V. Yours truly,
"December 2, 1862. ALEX. GREGG.
"Rev. C. GILLETTE."

"MY DEAR BISHOP: Will you be kind enough to give me, in writing, your reasons for not wishing Mr. Brown to do missionary duty? Will you also inform me whether you would consent that either of us should hold service and preach, if we were traveling in any part of the diocese where there was no congregation, and were desired so to do? Yours truly,
"AUSTIN, December 8, 1862. C. GILLETTE."

"AUSTIN, December 8, 1862.

"DEAR BROTHER GILLETTE: God forbid that I should not wish any clergyman of the Church to do missionary duty! Our recent conversation related to another point, as did others previously held, namely, my unwillingness for yourself and Mr. Brown, elsewhere than in this parish and its adjunct, to omit the words, "which has been forced upon us," in the prayer first put forth by me to be used during the present war. As to this, I supposed there had been of late so clear an understanding between us, as to preclude the necessity of any further inquiry or communication on the subject. I will, however, once more state, that I am not willing, by extending the limits of the permission, granted under peculiar circumstances, at your own and Mr. Brown's special request, to encroach further on the uniformity of prayer, and unity of devotion in the diocese, to disturb in other places, under any circumstances, the peace of the Church in this matter, or wound afresh the deepest sensibilities of our people, who, with very few exceptions, regard the voluntary omission of said words as vitally touching the justice and righteousness of this war of defense against a ruthlessly invading foe, and as indicative of a want of sympathy in our cause. If there was any error of judgment at the first, as many appear to think, in granting the permission at all, let the unhappy effects, which we have here painfully experienced, be extended no further.

"Yours truly in Christ,   ALEX. GREGG.
"Rev. C. GILLETTE."

The Bishop returned thanks for certain confederate victories, to which he did not hear me say Amen, and took me to task concerning it, on which account I addressed him as follows:

"MY DEAR BISHOP: I was very much astonished at the question you propounded to me at the vestry-room, on Wednesday, seventh instant, as well as at the manner of propounding it. In reflecting upon it since, my astonishment has not abated, and I desire to learn whether you asked the question, supposing you had authority as my Bishop so to do, or whether you asked it as a friend, and merely to satisfy curiosity? It is scarcely necessary for me to add, that I feel deeply wounded at such a question asked in such a way.

"Yours truly, "CHARLES GILLETTE.
"AUSTIN, Jan. 14, 1863."

"AUSTIN, Jan. 15, 1863.

"DEAR BROTHER GILLETTE: To your note of yesterday touching the question referred to, namely, the painful impression left on my mind that you had not responded to the special thanksgivings offered by me for the Confederate victories at Fredericksburgh and Galveston respectively, was correct; I reply, that it was propounded by me in the same capacity, precisely, in which both oral and written communications have been received and replied to from you as Rector of St. David's, touching the difficulties that have arisen, and the questions at issue of late.

"I meant to claim no such authority in asking the question as to make an answer from you obligatory; and yet felt then, as I do now, that it was altogether proper under the circumstances, and in connection with what has transpired between us.

"I must confess my surprise at the feeling of astonishment to which you give expression. It did not so strike me at the time.

"I did not mean or wish to wound you, and was unconscious of any thing offensive in my tone or manner, though aware, of course, that it would be an unpleasant question to you. It was painful to me, I assure you, to approach you on such a subject, as has been the trial to my feelings in St. David's for some time past. Yours truly, "ALEX. GREGG.
"Rev. C. GILLETTE."

"MY DEAR BISHOP: Your note of yesterday does not relieve my mind from doubt concerning the position you design to occupy. My desire is to learn a simple fact, clearly stated by yourself. And I desire to learn this fact as a guide in the performance of what may seem to me to be duty. Neither of us ought to fear a clear statement of truth. I desire, therefore, that you will inform me plainly, whether you asked the question before referred to, supposing you had authority as my Bishop so to do?

"To my mind, there is a wide difference between having authority to ask a question, and power to compel an answer. In the latter proposition I feel no special interest at present.

"I regret that there should have been any thing in St. David's to try your feelings. I have endeavored to cause you as little trouble as possible, and feel that, under the circumstances, I am not justly chargeable with blame. I have myself for a long time been deeply pained and grieved at the condition of things; and the more so, because I could discover no necessity for it. But the circumstances have been beyond my control, and, therefore, I do not consider myself responsible. Yours truly, CHARLES GILLETTE.
"AUSTIN, Jan. 17, 1863."

"AUSTIN, Jan. 17, 1863.

"DEAR BROTHER GILLETTE: I regarded my note of yesterday as sufficiently explicit; supposing it would convey a clear idea to your mind as to the position I meant to occupy in the matter referred to.

"If you think, as your language seems to import, that I fear 'a clear statement of truth' on the subject, you entirely misapprehend me, and have made an imputation which should be plainly alleged, or if not meant, at once withdrawn. I know not why I should fear to speak clearly. I may fail through inability to do so, but nothing more.

"As to the point upon which you desire to be informed plainly, namely, whether I asked the question supposing I had authority as your Bishop to do so; I answer, not such authority as is specifically conferred by canon in certain cases, or, in other words, the question was not asked in the highest sense authoritatively. It was simply in the exercise of the right, which a Bishop may be presumed to have, to approach his clergy by way of inquiry in matters affecting the individual or the Church; as to which suggestion may be made, advice given, or such other action taken, as may tend to the Church's welfare. In connection with the communications formerly made between us, the question should not have excited surprise.

"While there is a difference, as you remark, 'between having authority to ask a question and power to compel an answer,' you have strangely mistaken the purport of words—since the term 'obligatory' could scarcely be presumed in such a case to have been used in any other than its usual moral acceptation—one of those instances of obligation where the individual must judge for himself.

"It would be more than useless to discuss the question now, as to whom responsibility properly attaches for the state of things existing in this parish. There is no reason to hope that there ever will be an agreement of opinion between the parties immediately concerned, or those whose feelings so widely differ in regard to the great struggle now convulsing the country.

"The sympathies cherished and opinions entertained (for they rise far above what is merely political) will never, perhaps, be materially changed! Whether in Church or State, account must be given to God for all that has transpired.

"Yours truly, ALEX. GREGG.
"Rev. C. GILLETTE."

"MY DEAR BISHOP: I am obliged to you for your clear statement of your position in your last note. I am probably a little dull of comprehension, and need more explicit language than most persons.

"I did not intend to cast any imputation by the language used by me in my last communication. This statement I trust will be satisfactory on that point.

"You say: 'It was simply in the exercise of the right which a Bishop may be presumed to have to approach his clergy by way of inquiry in matters affecting the individual or the Church, as to which suggestion may be made, advice given, or such other action taken, as may tend to the Church's welfare.'

"According to the first fact of this statement, it may be readily conceded that a Bishop has a right in many things to question his clergy, where he thinks 'suggestion may be made, or advice given.' But it may also be readily conceived that a Bishop may overstep the bounds of his prerogative, and question in matters where conscience is concerned, and over which he can have no jurisdiction nor any right to question.

"As to the case where prayer is offered in the worshiping assembly, who but God is to judge in regard to the purity of intention, or the rectitude of conduct in any individual, in saying, or omitting to say Amen, to any prayer offered, and what human being shall take it upon himself to judge his brother in such a matter, and pronounce it ' a grave offense,' when he does not say Amen audibly?

"If an individual offend in such a case, it seems to me he is clearly amenable to God, and to God alone. He may err, but it is an error where his brother has no right to intrude. 'To his own master he standeth or falleth.'

"I may not understand what is meant by the language, 'or such other action taken as may tend to the Church's welfare,' for it seems to me vague and indefinite; but I can hardly conceive that a Bishop has authority over his clergy, beyond that of counsel and advice, unless there has been some violation of canon law, or ordination vows.

"As you remark, ' it would be more than useless to discuss the question now, as to whom responsibility properly attaches,' etc. After all that had been said, I deem it but justice to myself as a minister in God's church, acting, as I humbly trust, in his fear, and praying to him for guidance and direction, to state that I do not feel the responsibility to rest with me. I occupy the position I do not of my own choice, nor is it one of my own seeking. It 'has been forced upon me, and I think without just cause.

"I feel that this matter has assumed a form 'far above what is merely political.' For, with all due deference, and without any design to be in the least disrespectful, I look upon it now as a settled design to force my conscience, or to drive me from the Diocese, if no harsher means are employed. And I pray God, in whose hands are the hearts of all, to overrule for his glory; if it must be by my suffering, His will be done.

"I trust I am not now acting, neither have heretofore acted, without a deep sense of my accountability to Him.

      "Yours truly,   "CHARLES GILLETTE.
"AUSTIN, January 19, 1863."

"AUSTIN, January 21, 1863.

"DEAR BROTHER GILLETTE: Your disavowal of any intention to cast an imputation on me, was satisfactory.

"While it is not at all pleasant to me to protract such a correspondence, I feel that it is proper for me to reply briefly to some of the remarks made in your note of yesterday. My statement was clear to you except the last clause, 'or such other action taken as may tend to the Church's welfare,' which you think is vague and indefinite.

"It was expressed, I admit, in very general terms, and meant to cover a class of cases which I thought it unnecessary to specify. Enough has been said which was definite.

"In the case supposed by you, where to question is to infringe, or to overstep the bounds of lawful prerogative, that is, the omitting to respond to a prayer, where it is a point of conscience between a man and his God, it may be so in the case of an individual in a strictly private capacity, but not of necessity when he is acting officially, and his course may involve, more or less, the welfare of a parish, the good of the Church. Here the Bishop may with propriety question for the purpose of making suggestion, or giving advice, or for the relief of his own mind, if painfully impressed by his brother's course. The plea of conscience must not be carried too far as a shield from inquiry. I need not remind you what trouble 'conscience' has given individuals or brought upon the world. Your general proposition, therefore, must be received with much qualification. In the case before us, where I could not but be impressed with the fact that you had not responded to certain special thanksgivings, was it not proper for me to question with a view to suggestion, advice, or my own relief and satisfaction—not desiring wantonly to intrude, or to indulge a harsh or censorious spirit—and especially was it not so in view of what had already transpired?

"You again remark, that you do not 'feel the responsibility to rest with you,' and add 'that the position you occupy has been forced upon you, and that without cause.' How forced, if you could at once have left, or afterward, when the President gave opportunity, or, indeed, at any time subsequent? If you chose to remain after a prayer had been put forth by your Bishop to which you could not assent, how can you say your position has been forced upon you? Or in choosing to omit certain words, (which was permitted at your request,) did you not take very high moral ground against this war of defense on our part, in opposition, as you well knew, to the prevailing sentiment in the Diocese? Was the position forced upon you? But, thus remaining and protesting thus, as often as you read the prayer,—and that in a leading parish and the capital of the State, with not a few around you sympathizing in your course, and known to be disaffected toward the government, protesting thus against the war, though one of holy defense and sacred justice on our part,—the action of the Convention was not only timely and proper, but imperiously demanded! and can you say that action or its legitimate results was forced upon you? When afterward it became proper, as the Convention requested to read the extract from my address, with the report and resolutions of the Committee, did you not choose to defer the reading because of a very unsound and unpatriotic feeling on a part of the congregation? Do you suppose that in any other parish, or locality in the Diocese, it would have driven any from the communion? Instead of the matter referred to, did you not choose to preach a sermon which, however proper in itself, became a source of offense to not a few, because of its evident bearing on the existing state of things? When afterward a brother clergyman came to the parish, who had been prominent in the action taken by the Convention, did courtesy call for more than a general invitation for him to officiate for you, without pressing him for his reasons in declining? Was not the conversation in the vestry-room, afterward, requested by yourself, and did not the papers subsequently submitted by you, elicit my communication in reply; and the correspondence since, has it not been induced by you in the first instance? May it not be that, unconsciously to yourself, you have been led to seek the attitude of an injured and persecuted man? and I say this in no spirit of unkindness, or to reflect on your sincerity.

"*What, then,* has been forced upon you? What has led, step by step, to all that has transpired? When you saw in the outset that the position you were about to take would *array* you against the *Diocese* in a matter where the deepest and most sacred feelings were involved—for this was actually the case—how could you expect the plea of conscience to relieve you of the consequent responsibility, and so to change the whole order and aspect of things, as to make that position and its results forced upon yourself?

"A man in an official position, and such as you have occupied in the Diocese, could not expect to be regarded in the light of a mere private individual; and this appears to me one of the serious errors into which you have fallen.

"You furthermore remark: 'I look upon it now as a settled design to force my conscience, or drive me from the Diocese if no harsher measures are employed.'

"This allegation is not, in my opinion, at all supported by the facts in the case, and you can not take the position, which you doubtless believe yourself to occupy, of an injured and persecuted man. I say this most emphatically! What you mean by 'harsher measures' I do not exactly comprehend. If you refer to violent proceedings against your person, I feel sure you would not for a moment imagine, that I have ever thought of, or would countenance in the slightest degree, any thing of the kind, or that there are any who would. Let me also assure you that such a thing as forcing your conscience has never been thought of. God forbid that it should be so!

"As to 'a settled design to drive you from the Diocese,' while it is a *hard saying*, let me remark, and I do it in sorrow of heart, that what has transpired in consequence of the position first taken by you, and naturally tending to that point, namely, your leaving sooner or later, as you remarked to me some time since you expected to do so, must not by any means be confounded with a design on the part of others to drive you off. That first position set you adrift on the current of events; and however pure your intentions, or satisfied in your mind of the rectitude of your course, (for thus I believe you have felt and acted,) yet *such was that position* and your *subsequent course*, that deep and general feeling has been excited both here and elsewhere through the Diocese; and nothing has occurred to my knowledge, by any open expression of feeling or sentiment on your part, to lessen that feeling. The view expressed by you, too, respecting your brethren, that 'their action partook largely of an intolerant, sectarian, and persecuting spirit,' and 'that they were proposing a new test of fitness for ministerial labor among them hitherto unknown in the Church, saying, you must believe with us politically, or we can not fraternize with you; but we will by our action publicly say, you are unworthy to labor with us as a minister in the Church of God'—all this indicated that you could not, with satisfaction to yourself, remain permanently among them, and that it might be best that you should not. But *from whence has such a state* of things proceeded? Does it necessarily follow, that because one or two are in conflict with a larger number, or have placed themselves in conflict, that the latter are in the wrong and the former injured and persecuted?

"In declining to officiate for you, your brethren who have been here did it of their own free will and accord, and simply on the ground that in the position you had taken with reference to the prayer they could not ask you to officiate for them, and they would much have preferred that so unpleasant an issue should not have been forced upon them. In declining to extend the permission to omit the words in the prayer in other places than this parish and its adjunct, I stated the reasons which influenced me, and they are such as my judgment approves.

"But what more need be said? I have most devoutly wished and earnestly prayed, that the course of this world might be so peaceably ordered by God's government, that his Church might joyfully serve him in all godly quietness through Jesus Christ our Lord. And in my official course, since our national troubles commenced, I have only sought to discharge, in the fear of God, what I conceived to be my duty at this momentous crisis, both to Church and State, for the two *are now* and ever *will be* closely and indissolubly connected. I have feared from the first that you did not fully realize the true character of this war, the issue at stake, the spirit and design of our enemies, the unalterable determination on the part of our people that the Government from which they separated should never be reëstablished over them, and the feeling which the non-avowal of sympathy with them in their perilous struggle would naturally excite in their hearts. But enough of this!

"I write in sorrow, and God knoweth the feelings of my heart. In no spirit of unkindness has a word been uttered. There has been much in the past to bind me to you in the ties of Christian affection, and I shall never cease to pray for the happiness and welfare of you and yours.

"May God be with us both, to direct us in these, as in all our doings, with his most gracious favor! Whatever the course of things may be hereafter, whatever our trials—for we must expect to be tried—may it only be to incite us to the more faithful discharge of duty here, and the laying up a sure and immutable crown of rejoicing hereafter.

"Yours truly, ALEX. GREGG.
"Rev. C. GILLETTE."

"MY DEAR BISHOP: Your communication of yesterday is so long that my engagements will not permit my answering it to-day. If it please God, I will answer it on your return from your visitation. Yours truly,
"CHARLES GILLETTE.
"AUSTIN, Jan. 22, 1863."

"MY DEAR BISHOP: I do not suppose this correspondence can be any more pleasant to me than to yourself. I have entered upon it, and pursued it, only as a matter of self-defense and for the vindication of the Church and my order of the ministry.

"Your reasoning is to me very strange, but with your avowal of the close and indissoluble connection of the Church and State now and ever, I think I understand you.

"This union I neither see nor acknowledge, and I can only suppose you are mistaken in your statement. But let me take up some of the points in your communication in nearly the order in which they are mentioned.

"In regard to the language of your former communication, 'or such other action,' etc., you say you 'expressed it in general terms, and meant it to cover a class of cases,' etc. I am utterly at a loss to know to what class of cases you refer, as I conceive the whole ground covered by the first part of your statement, and by the canon law of the Church—when a bishop has exhausted his counsel and advice, I conceive he has nothing more to do, until it comes to canon law. I can, therefore, see no cases covered, and no cases that *could be covered* by the language used. Most undoubtedly a bishop is bound by law, as well as his clergy, and there are very few cases where 'the Church's welfare is concerned,' that he can become a law unto himself or to them.

"In regard to saying *amen*, let me state the individual case. You twice returned thanks for victories. You were under the impression that I did not say amen to either, and you asked me if I did. In reply I stated that for one I did say amen, for the other I did not, and I gave you my reasons. This I did as a matter of friendship, not because I acknowledged any right in you, as my Bishop, to ask the question, or any obligation on me as your presbyter to answer it. I make no objection to answering the question as a friend, but I utterly refuse to answer it when asked authoritatively. I claim that any minister, when another is officiating, is simply an individual worshiper, and is no more responsible to his Bishop, for saying amen to a prayer or a thanksgiving, than any member of the congregation. He is not acting officially, but as an individual, and God alone has the right to take cognizance of his acts. It is a matter of conscience between him and his God, and no individual man has a right to intrude. This general proposition *must be received, I think, without qualification*, and covers the point at issue in the present correspondence. But as some important points in regard to what has passed during the last year and a half are brought forward, I propose to refer to them.

"In regard to my position being forced upon me, you ask how, and then enumerate a series of acts of mine, all tending, as you judge, to bring me into my present position, and hence you conclude, that I alone have been in fault, and I alone am responsible; as if all these had been the deliberate acts and choice of myself—a choice, too, with the consequences full before me. It would be very easy to refute all this by a supposed case, for it all goes to show how an opinion entertained makes every thing right on one side, and not entertained makes every thing wrong on the other side. But it will be sufficient for present purposes to take a plain statement of facts.

"Before entering the sacred ministry, my mind was turned upon the different fields of labor calling for the services of clergymen; I took a survey of work at home and abroad, and considered the subject attentively for several years, while preparing for my future work. Texas was then a foreign field, and to me far less inviting than any of those occupied by the Church, except Africa. As a matter of choice, I would sooner have gone at that time to Greece, or Syria, or China, than to Texas.

"When ordained, I was urged to stay at home among known and tried friends; inducements were held out to me such as would have secured competence and comparative ease. But I felt it an imperative duty to pass all these by, and go where comparatively none would go—for only two of our clergymen were then in this vast field. I therefore came to Texas, not as a matter of choice, but of duty—a conscientious feeling of duty from which I dared not turn away. Thus was my field of labor in the Church fixed—forced upon me, if you choose—by that troublesome conscience *whose voice I dared not disregard.*

"For twenty years my poor services have been given to the Church in Texas: given with the same feeling, that in the providence of God here was my lot, and that I might not go elsewhere. That same 'troublesome conscience' forces me to stand in my lot, *through evil* as well as *good report.* But if I now felt myself free to seek another place of abode and labor in God's vineyard, and if there were no hindrances from the powers that be, as you suppose, (which supposition admits of great doubt,) still my present position is forced upon me by the necessities of the case. I have a family of helpless children dependent upon my daily exertions for bread. I have no money, and have never had, since in Texas, more than sufficient to meet my constantly recurring wants. I have no pecuniary interest anywhere but here. The small amount of property I have, if sold to-day at a full valuation, would do little more than pay my debts and take my family out of the country. But it is patent to you, and to every one, that no sale of property could now be effected, for money which could be used beyond the limits of the Confederacy, nor could this have been done at any time since the troubles commenced. If, then, I desired ever so much to go, and there was nothing in the way but the want of means, how could I go, unless I were to turn myself and family into a set of beggars and live upon the charity of those we might find willing to give? Would there be any thing in such a course which would seem to be following the leadings of God's providence? You being judge, is there any thing in the necessities of the case which would justify such a course? And by so doing would I not justly come under the condemnation of the Apostle, when he says, 'He that provideth not for his own, and especially for those of his own household, hath denied the faith, and is worse than an infidel'? The present state of things which makes it a pecuniary impossibility for me to make a change, has been brought about without my seeking or my aiding; hence, in this respect, my present position · has been forced upon me.'

"But when I said my position was 'forced upon me,' I meant something more than mere locality—I meant the position I occupy before the public. And here let me remark that my position was the same in this respect as now, before most of the things transpired which are mentioned in your communication, and for which you think me censurable. There has been no material change of which I am aware.

"What is this position? It is a feeling in the public mind that I have arrayed myself in opposition to my Bishop and to my brethren of the clergy. Is this true as a matter of fact? I think not. How, then, do I come to occupy this position? I answer, from misunderstanding and misrepresentation. Not that I charge any one with willfully doing me injustice; but it has so happened that there has not been a clear understanding of the case. What have been the facts? Simply this: My Bishop set forth a prayer in which there occurs, not as a petition, but as a declaration of a matter of fact, a political opinion —an opinion which, if it were necessary to maintain, it certainly need not have been made a subject of information to the Almighty in a prayer composed for public use in the Church—an opinion concerning which there was bound to be diversity. In this opinion I frankly stated to my Bishop, in the outset, that I conscientiously differed with him, and asked his permission to omit the declaration in using the prayer. The omission affected not in the slightest degree a single petition in the prayer. In asking to be excused from declaring the opinion, I did not seek to force my opinion upon any body else. I only asked to be excused from declaring before God, in prayer, that to be a fact which I was not convinced was a fact. Surely, under such circumstances, I only asked what was lawful for me to ask, and what, as an honest Christian man, I was bound to ask; and in granting my request, my Bishop only did what I think a wise, considerate, Christian Bishop would always do. Thus far I can see nothing wrong. A difference of opinion on the point in question was lawful. It was lawful and right, under the circumstances, for me to ask to be excused from declaring the opinion. It was lawful for my Bishop to excuse me, and here the matter might and, in my judgment, ought to have ended. Did it so end? Far from it. Although my Bishop said (though he would not now repeat it) 'that had the matter been suggested to him before the printing of the prayer, he would have omitted the words in question,' and although he now declares that 'taken without these words, those who have been most decided in the expression of opinion on the subject have admitted that the prayer would yet be suitable and comprehensive, and cover the ground generally which such a prayer should do,' although, under these circumstances, it could be no matter of conscience with him to have the words used, he still claims the right, whenever present, to read the prayer himself with the words, and finds fault with me for not saying amen. He persists in this Sunday after Sunday, although he is aware that not only myself, but many communicants in the congregation are wounded by its use, and can not say amen. The Bishop himself thus breaks the unity of worship in a Christian congregation. For if the unity of worship so much talked of be broken, it must be broken in a single congregation. For it is not probable that all the congregations in one Diocese, to say nothing of a more extended region, use precisely the same prayers, no more and no less, on any given Sunday. Am I not forced, then, to occupy the position I now do, by the constantly recurring act of my Bishop, who might have freed me from it without any violation of conscience by permitting the prayer to be used always in the same way in the same congregation? It is highly probable, if this had been done from the beginning, the change would never have been observed, and all the feeling which has been manifested would have been avoided. I did not seek or desire to express any opinion upon the point in question. If I have done so, it is because I have been forced to do it in a negative manner, by asking to be excused from uttering, as a fact, that which I could not see reason to believe was true.

"Again, if I have only done what my Bishop gave me leave to do—which leave he had a perfect right to give, and so have in no way placed myself in opposition to him, nor in any way transgressed any law or regulation of the Church—have I not further been forced into the position I occupy by the action of my brethren in the Convention, whereby they proclaim to the world that I am guilty of grave offenses, so grave that I must not be permitted to hold any place in the management of the affairs of the Diocese; but my name must be stricken from every committee and every office, although I had spent all my ministerial life in Texas, wearing myself out for the good of the Church, having participated in all the councils of the Church since the organization of the Diocese, there being only one presbyter who has spent half the time in Texas that I have done? Was not the public mind still further prejudiced by the Convention's passing a series of resolutions, and requesting them to be read in all the congregations, with the intent, as a brother informed me, of 'making me define my position, politically'? And has it not still further been forced upon me by my brethren, who have visited here, refusing to officiate for me, thus giving the world to understand that I am guilty of such grave offenses that they could not fellowship with me? And have not all these things been with the knowledge and consent of my Bishop? Surely, if a position, unsought and undesired, was ever forced upon a man, mine has been forced upon me, and, as I still think, without my having given any cause; for, I can not suppose that any would be so unreasonable as to say I had given occasion for all this, when I had simply used a plain right to ask to be excused from uttering a political sentiment in public prayer, simply as a matter of information to the Almighty, which statement I did not see reason to believe to be strictly true, and my Bishop had granted my request, excusing me from making the assertion.

"In regard to forcing my conscience, driving me from the Diocese, or using harsher means, the simple facts seem to me to be these: It may be my misfortune not to see points as clearly as some others, but so it was, that I did not, and do not now, see what others said they did, and I asked to be excused from declaring the same, on the ground of conscientious scruple. Other very serious grounds of objection might be found to using the assertion in a public prayer. But the ground of conscience was that on which I honestly asked to be excused. I am 'aware of the trouble conscience has given individuals and brought upon the world.' But because conscience has been abused, I do not see that *that* excuses a man for having no conscience, or disregarding it, when he has one. Having conscience as the ground for asking the excuse, being excused by my Bishop on that ground, what is it but an attempt to force my conscience when I am constantly made to feel, by the premeditated acts of my brethren, that they are holding me up before the public as one unworthy to associate with them, thus bringing the outside pressure of an over-excited public to bear, either to make me yield and use the words, contrary to my own convictions of right, or else leave the Diocese? What is it but an attempt to force my conscience, or drive me from the Diocese, when I am forbidden to hold even an occasional service anywhere in the Diocese out of my own parish, although persons having no minister might desire me to give them the services of the Church? What means the invitation I have several times had, to leave the Diocese, by those who think they can judge of what is my duty in this matter better than I can myself, and who seem to think that for a minister to change his place of labor in the Church he has only to will a change, and make it without reference to any surroundings except the wish of those who may desire to be rid of his company? As the whole matter turns on a point of conscience, how could it be expected that any 'open expression of feeling or sentiment' of mine should be given to change the sentiment of others toward me, unless I violated my conscience? Could I utter as truth what I did not believe to be true, without violating my conscience? As in the dilemma in which I am placed, only the two alternatives are offered me—of leaving the Diocese, or using the words; what is it but a settled attempt to force my conscience or drive me from the Diocese?

"In regard to harsher means, let me state facts. The public are much excited, and seem determined that all, even ministers, shall share largely in their excitement. Many acts of violence, without process of law, have been committed. If I am rightly informed, at least a hundred and fifty men in this State have lost their lives since these troubles commenced, without any legal tribunal having determined that they had violated the laws of the land. It is a fact well known to all living in this vicinity that there has been, at times, intense excitement among the masses of the people; and it only needed a spark to have kindled a flame which no human skill or foresight could have controlled or seen the end of.

"Once started it would have been a mob uncontrolled, and only to cease when the frenzy should have worn itself out. Under such circumstances, who could tell where the blow would fall, or who would have been the victim? Is it not evident that those who, from any cause, had been made prominent, whether by their own acts or the acts of others, would be most likely to suffer from the unrestrained violence of the mob? Has there not been reason, then, for men who have been evil spoken of to fear the hand of violence and 'harsher means'?

"In regard to the extending the permission to hold service elsewhere, if I should be out of my parish, and requested so to do by a minister, or by a congregation without a minister, I must say in all candor, though with great sorrow, that I think you have entirely exceeded your authority in the case, and that there is no canon law of the Church which will sustain a Bishop in such a prohibition, not even in the letter, and certainly not in the spirit.

"You say, 'the Church and State are now and ever will be closely and indissolubly connected.' As this language is generally understood, I must beg to differ from the statement here made. I think the Church and State are separate and distinct, and I trust will ever so remain. But with such an opinion entertained, I can easily conceive how your mind has been greatly biased in this whole matter, and that a supposed offense against the State may be punishable in the Church, and that a political opinion must be made an article of faith; for the whole of this proceeding seems to me to look directly to this, and nothing less. I have heard you accused of seeking the union of Church and State, under the Confederacy, which I have hitherto denied, and I sincerely regret that your own language puts it out of my power to do this any more.

"Whatever may be your ability satisfactorily to disavow the assumption which you claim, 'that there is a connection between Church and State,' or that such connection is designed or intended to be established, yet allow me to suggest that the use of such language is calculated to do more injury, both to our Church and the liberal State which gives free toleration to every persuasion of Christians, and to every character of religionists, than any other which man can invent. The language is precisely that employed in the constitutions and laws of the despotic governments, where such a connection, in fact, exists—a connection which has furnished as martyrs tens of thousands of dissenters and non-conformists. Whatever difference of opinion there may be in regard to the present unfortunate and unhappy contest, I do not believe that any considerable number of either party regarded as the smallest boon won by our Protestant fathers, that they forever severed the political connection between Church and State. Nothing could now be a severer blow to the cause which you have so much at heart than the publicity of the sentiments that such connection has never, in fact, been dissolved, but that it still exists in theory and in fact. I am persuaded that misapprehensions upon a question so vital to civil and religious liberty have been at the foundation of the acts of yourself and the Bishops of the other Dioceses, which have caused the imputation in some quarters that the Episcopal Church desired a legal recognition as the Church of the Confederate States of America.

"I can easily conceive such views, when hypothetically entertained, as connection between Church and State, can lead to the great mistake, that Christian ministers should enter into the political contests of the day. This interference in public affairs by the pulpits of the North is everywhere conceded to have been a principal element which has led to the terrible civil war which now scourges the land. I can not admit such connections between Church and State, hence my conscientious belief, that it is the duty of Christian ministers to know 'only Christ, and him crucified.' The affairs and management of the State belong to the people and to the Governors of their choice. Our clergy, unlike the Bishops of England, have no place in the civil government; any assumptions to the contrary are only apples of discord, and he who maintains them will be found, ere long, scattering 'firebrands, arrows, and death.'

"There are a few things alluded to in your communication which, perhaps, need some words of explanation on my part. You speak of 'your delay to read the resolutions of the Convention, and of the sermon preached on that occasion.' I did not suppose then, nor do I suppose now, that the reading of the resolutions one Sunday sooner or later made the slightest difference. It so happened that the resolutions reached me two or three days before Communion Sunday. I saw from the character of the resolutions that in my congregation their being read would produce unpleasant feeling, and I felt certain would keep some from the Communion. I, therefore, judged it more prudent to defer reading them to another Sunday, and told you so when you asked me if I intended to read them on that day. When you insisted that you would go into my pulpit and read them on that day, if I did not, I told you that you had no right to do so; that you were bound by the same laws that regulated any presbyter in my parish, except when on a visitation. When you insisted that you had a right, in virtue of its being your parish church, (by which I suppose you meant the parish in which you resided,) I told you, that if you persisted I should not have the Communion, and you finally yielded. I thought I was the best judge in my own parish. I was not responsible for the state of feeling in my parish at the time, but as a faithful pastor it was my duty to see how it might best be met.

"In regard to the sermon preached on that occasion, I think it was entirely in accordance with the Gospel. It was prepared and preached, word for word the same, six years before, and therefore could have had no special reference to any thing then transpiring. If any supposed otherwise, does it not show that it must have been in the imagination of the listener, or else that such a sermon was timely and needed? I have never, up to this time, heard any one express any dissatisfaction with the sermon, nor have I heard any one, except yourself, say that any dissatisfaction was expressed. You heard the discourse, and stated to me afterward that there was nothing in the sermon itself that any one could find fault with.

"You speak of my pressing a brother for his reasons for not officiating for me. I did not intend to be discourteous in what I did. His answer to my invitation was such that I thought he rather desired to give me his reason for refusing, and I was somewhat confirmed in this idea by learning afterward that he had given the same information, unasked, to a member of the Church who had simply been introduced to him.

"You say: 'When you saw in the outset the position you were about to take would array you against the Diocese.' This is certainly very strange language, under the circumstances. I did not suppose that any one foresaw what has followed in this connection. In a conversation had with yourself, I understood you to say, that you had no idea at the time the permission was asked, of what has followed. I certainly foresaw nothing of the kind, nor did I dream of arraying myself against any one, or that any would array themselves against me, which I am sorry to find seems now to be the case.

"You speak of my remarking to you 'some time since that

I expected to leave the Diocese.' You certainly mistook my meaning. I remarked to you that certain things would 'drive me from the Diocese;' not at all that I expected to go of my own free will and accord. I think you will easily call to mind the circumstances under which these remarks were made. I grieve to say it, but it was when I felt deeply wounded at what seemed plain to me, and I thought ought to have been plain to my Bishop—that, without intending it, he was fostering a spirit of dissension among my congregation; for he had just returned from performing the funeral services in the family of one of my parishioners, which he had done without saying a word to me, except to send me word a little before the time of service, that he was going to do it. I have felt that by this, and by other acts of my Bishop, my hands were weakened in my parish, and that dissensions were cherished and breaches made wider. And it was in view of such things that I said, I could see plainly that these things would drive me from the Diocese.

"You say, again, 'I have feared from the first that you did not fully realize the true character of this war,' etc. I confess that from the first I have felt it quite enough for me to faithfully perform the duties of my station as a Christian minister, without mingling in any way with the excited feeling which I see around, and growing out of a state of war. A Christian minister may see and lament the evils attendant on such a state of things as now exists; but how he, as an ambassador of the Prince of Peace, the herald of Him who would 'neither strive, nor cry, nor cause his voice to be heard in the streets'—how he can come down from his high calling, to mingle and make himself one in these earthly conflicts, I do not understand. I have not so learned Christ.

"As proof that this is no new opinion with me, I may appeal to my whole life. Before I left the land of my nativity, the practice of preachers carrying political opinions into the pulpit had become so frequent as to threaten Christian fraternity and social relations. I had always understood our Church to deplore and condemn, even this assumed connection between Church and State; and when I entered the sacred ministry I had a fixed determination never to mingle politics with the

Gospel of Christ. When I came to Texas, I found a free people, living under a constitution which guaranteed a separate nationality, and rejoicing in nothing more than that the revolution of 1836 had forever separated that 'connection between Church and State,' which had led and still leads to such disturbing 'pronunciamentos,' and to such frequently recurring bloodshed, in the republic from which they had severed their political connection; I here found our Church under the missionary patronage, and joined by religious connection with the Church of the United States. One year after my arrival in Texas, a civil revolution commenced, which merged the nationality of Texas in that of the United States. In this revolution I took no part beyond the casting of a vote, feeling it then, as now, my duty 'to render unto Cæsar the things that are Cæsar's, and to God the things that are God's.' Historians say that the consummation of this revolution 'forced' a war, but upon whom the war was forced, God alone can judge—I did not feel it my duty, nor did our Church then undertake to decide by whom, or upon whom 'the war was forced.' It certainly severed the 'connection of Church and State,' in a vast field which it opened to our labors. The revolution in which we now find ourselves may be beyond my comprehension; I own that I regard it as a matter of inscrutable Providence. But I feel in my heart that it brings no new political 'connection between Church and State.' It makes no new change in the duties of a Christian minister. We have yet in the Church very much land to be possessed. A vast field for religious work is before us. I own it to be the duty of us all, as citizens, to submit to the powers that be, to observe the constitution and laws which are intended to operate upon all alike, to acknowledge political changes as established facts. But whether these changes have been 'forced' or voluntary, wise or unwise, for the happiness of the people, or to make it more burdensome upon them, are matters which, in my humble judgment, neither Bishop, Priest Deacon, or Convention can determine at the outset. Neither the Constitution, law, nor the Bible punishes or authorizes human punishment for non-conformity in political or religious sentiments. To claim it, is to claim absolute power. To practice it and assert it on the ground of the 'connection of Church and State,' certainly tends to the overthrow of both, just in proportion to the influence of those who assert and act upon the hypothesis.

"You say, again, 'Does it necessarily follow, that, because one or two are in conflict with a larger number, or have placed themselves in conflict, that the latter are in the wrong, and the former injured and persecuted?' I answer no—nor is the converse of the proposition of necessity true. I am not aware that any one has made or maintained the proposition here stated. Again, you say: 'You can not take the position, which you doubtless believe yourself to occupy, of an injured and persecuted man.' In regard to this assertion, I suppose it would only be a matter of opinion between us, after all that might be said upon the subject. But if he whose rights are interfered with without cause, whose character and influence is assailed without just reason, whose honest labors in the most sacred profession are curtailed and his influence well-nigh lost for the time being—and all this too for the sake of an opinion, an opinion he does not seek to express, but only desires not to express its opposite,—if such an one is not injured and persecuted, then I think it would be hard to tell what injury and persecution mean. That a man does not utter the words dictated to him in solemn prayer, which express simply the declaration of an opinion which he can see no ground for believing true, and from the utterance of which he has been excused by the individual dictating—that for this he should be proscribed, and his name cast out as evil,—if it be not persecution, what is it? It is more than useless to say such an one has set himself in opposition. How set himself in opposition, when he has simply exercised the right of having an opinion, has done nothing more than exercise liberty of conscience, and if he is made to suffer in any way for this, what is it but being injured and persecuted? The opposite reasoning from this would justify all the persecuting powers which have ever existed, and at once bring us to a point when we must say that no persecution for conscience's sake has ever existed. The poor man who has suffered martyrdom for opinion's sake, has not been persecuted or injured; he set himself in opposition to a majority by holding an opinion contrary to theirs, and he has no right to have an opinion of his own, even if he did not seek to express it. Therefore, no matter what may have happened to him, he has not been persecuted and injured; his life even was a just forfeiture of his having an opinion. I am sure that my Bishop would give his assent to no such reasoning as this, and yet, when carefully considered and carried out, I can see only this end to which it would lead. It seems to me the very form that every persecuting and fanatical spirit has taken, from the commencement of the world downward. My view of this subject may be wrong, but it is the only view which *seems* to me correct.

' "You expressed a desire not to continue this correspondence. I have consequently dwelt more at length on some points mentioned in your last communication than I otherwise should. I do not feel that the subject is by any means exhausted, but I may weary your patience by writing further.

"Allow me to say, in conclusion, that no word which I have uttered here has been dictated by the slightest unkind feeling toward yourself or any one else. I have simply endeavored to make myself understood in matters where I consider the greatest and dearest principles involved—principles which rise far, *very far*, 'above mere political opinion.' I give you full credit for all honesty of purpose, but I feel that your idea of the 'connection of Church and State' has led you into error, and greatly biased your judgment in this whole matter.

"I most heartily and devoutly join you in the prayer, 'that the course of this world may be so peaceably ordered,' etc., and, again, 'that God may be with us both, to direct us in these and all our doings with his most gracious favor.' I also pray that our trials may incite us to the more faithful discharge of our duty here, and the laying up of a sure and immutable crown of rejoicing hereafter. Yours, truly,

"AUSTIN, March 16, 1863.   CHARLES GILLETTE."

"AUSTIN, April 20, 1863.

"DEAR BROTHER GILLETTE: The brief reply which I designed making to your communication of the sixteenth ultimo, has been delayed simply by the pressure of other work.

"To protract the correspondence can tend only to evil, involving as it does new questions or issues as to memory of facts, construction of language, the bearing of actions, etc., concerning *all which*, it is manifest, no better understanding will be reached. Nor, let it be added, can mere reïteration add force to what has once been said.

"I could say somewhat in reply to your undertaking to 'vindicate the Church,' and to inform me as to the rights and duties of a Bishop, but it would be unkind, and I forbear.

"The circumstances under which you came to Texas, though you dwell much on the subject, have really nothing to do with the present issue.

"Having taken the position of one persecuted, it would be worse than useless to discuss questions of conscience, or what constitutes persecution, or whether one may not be egregiously mistaken as to his own position in the premises.

"As to the point whether your present position has been forced upon you, the question is not whether you foresaw or any one else what followed, but simply, has it resulted, in the natural order of things, from the stand you first took. *You* think not, as was to be expected. Let it remain so, then, for enough has been said as to that.

"You say I claim the right to read the prayer! Certainly. Did you not unqualifiedly consent that I should always do so, when present? Was it not the distinct understanding? Why, then, complain so dolorously now? and why, in view of these facts, the *extraordinary assertion* that I violate unity in reading my own prayer? What unity? That of disaffection? of Northern sympathy? Are only one class to be regarded?

"Is it possible you can imagine, had you been quietly permitted to read the prayer yourself, that your omission of the words would not have been observed, or created feeling? or that there has been nothing else to lead to the general belief that your real sympathies have not been with us in this cruel and monstrous inroad of our enemies! Are ministers not men! and subjects of the State? And are they expected to reach such a sublimated point of virtue as to have no wish as to the result of a struggle like this? Does reason, does conscience, does religion forbid it in them? Have they not to renounce every noble sentiment of love of country, to be without ardent desire, though in submission to the will of God?

"You have made much ado about political excitement, etc., (though I know none of our clergy who have gone beyond the bounds of propriety in this matter,) as if this was a question of *politics!*

"You speak of one hundred and fifty citizens put to death in Texas, etc. I have kept no such accurate account! Do you include in the number of these, (all of whom you seem to consider political martyrs,) those who armed and organized themselves against the government, or were on their way to join the enemy? or, had gone, and returned to murder our people?

"You speak of law-abiding citizens here. Did you ever hear of any of this class who held out as long as they could against the payment of the war-tax?

"A Bishop may put forth prayers for extraordinary occasions; he may excuse the omission of certain words therein, in compliance with the request of one or more of the clergy! and yet, if he limits the bounds of that permission, territorially, for reasons which he may deem good, he at once becomes *despotic!* He must take the feelings of others as his guide! or incur severe censure! *Let this pass!*

"My repeated assertion, that there is an indissoluble connection between Church and State, alarms you! You once denied the charge above against me! that I desired an established religion. Alas! for me now, you can do so no more! My brother, your fancy has run away with you! The idea provokes a broad smile! I thought you understood the kind of moral connection referred to! None would be more surprised than the good Bishops of the Confederate States, who have shown themselves in this as true churchmen, as true patriots, at hearing of such grave apprehensions respecting them in a Texas Presbyter! For the quieting of your fears, let me tell you that I have, for more than a year past, been intending to give full expression to my views as to the relation of Church and State, etc., and I was actually engaged in doing so when your communication was handed to me. You will soon be able to consider these views at your leisure, and if you go beyond me in repudiating an established religion in any form, you will be radical indeed! To that document inquirers may after this be referred! I can readily conceive from whence the charge comes, that the Episcopal Church in this Diocese, or in the Confederacy, desires a union of Church and State. Let such a conceit be no more maintained!

"I still think you expressed yourself as first asserted by me in regard to leaving the Diocese—and am positive in my recollection!—but, like other issues, as to the memory of the fact, it must stand so!

"As to official acts performed by me in this parish, I utterly disclaim any intention or desire of injuring you, or fostering dissension. I said enough to you at the time in connection with every such act, and if that did not suffice to undeceive you of my feelings and motives in the matter, nothing I could now say would.

"I am not conscious in any instance of having violated the rules of propriety and courtesy. God forbid that I should trample on the rights of my brethren of the clergy! They are as dear to me as my own; but I have said enough to you on this subject in the past.

"It is not I who have fostered a feeling against you, tied your hands, or weakened your influence in this parish, but your own course, persistently maintained in different respects, from the beginning of these troubles! It is no pleasure to me, I assure you, to have to write thus. Justice to myself, however, demanded some reply; and it grieves me that such a communication should have been rendered proper!

"Yours truly, "ALEX GREGG.
"Rev. C. GILLETTE."

"MY DEAR BISHOP: Your communication of the twentieth instant, was handed me on the night of the twenty-first, after your departure for Houston.

"I have read it carefully, and find nothing in it which seems to me to pertain strictly to the questions at issue.

"I regret that you thought it 'proper' to return such an answer; but if you are satisfied with it, I do not complain.

"For the present, I forbear comments on your points of

departure from the main subject. Humbly praying that God may guide us both into the way of all truth, and lead us to accomplish that which shall be for his glory, I remain

"Yours truly,   CHARLES GILLETTE.

"AUSTIN, April 23, 1863."

"AUSTIN, May 22, 1863.

"DEAR BROTHER GILLETTE: Your brief note in reply to my communication of the twentieth ultimo. reached me at Houston. Lest my silence should be construed into an admission (which I am very far from making) of the correctness of your assertion, that there was nothing in my communication 'which pertained strictly to the questions at issue,' I need write simply to relieve you from any such impression. If there were 'points of departure from the main subject,' I only followed in your lead.

"I have neither the taste nor time, in such a correspondence, to reiterate the same things, to enter into vain disputes as to questions of fact, or to comment upon motives. That you should think my last a departure from the main subject is surprising indeed!

"In your prayer, that we may be guided into *all* truth, and led to accomplish *that* which shall be for God's glory, I heartily join—as in best wishes for your happiness. I remain

"Yours truly,   ALEX GREGG.

"Rev. C. GILLETTE."

The Bishop speaks in the foregoing letter of having kept no accurate account of murdered citizens. It seems that neither he nor I had kept a very accurate account, as Governor Hamilton states in his address to the people of Texas, issued about this time, that from our own public prints he had learned that, not only one hundred and fifty, but more than a thousand citizens of Texas had been murdered.

After the close of the Council in June, 1864, without any previous intimation of what he intended to do, or of what had been done, the Bishop sent me the following pastoral and note. As I was the only clergyman offending, it is hard to see the necessity of a public pastoral to withdraw the permission to omit the words in question, any more than to grant such permission, unless the object was to turn the attention of an excited public upon, and array them against, myself:

To the Clergy of the Protestant Episcopal Church in the Diocese of Texas:

"DEAR BRETHREN: I have had under careful consideration the 'Preamble and Resolution' adopted by our late Diocesan Council, (which will appear in the Journal,) most respectfully requesting me to withhold from every clergyman, or to withdraw, where it had been granted, permission to omit the words 'which has been forced upon us,' in the first special Prayer put forth to be used during the present war. This action, as those of you who were present are aware, was taken by the Council with the full understanding that it could only be suggestive or advisory, and that the Bishop would be as perfectly free as before to follow the dictates of his own judgment, it being left by canon a matter of right and responsibility exclusively with him. Since the adjournment of the Council, the clerical members of the Standing Committee, appointed by general Canon to be 'a Council of advice to the Bishop,' have also made a unanimous request to the same effect. The reasons set forth by the Council for its action are, the expediency and necessity of union and coöperation on the part of all at a time like the present; the fact that the omission of said words 'is a source of discord and contention,' and 'in its measure, subversive of truth, and love, and unity, and peace'—and, that the ignoring of such an historical fact vitally affects the responsibility involved as to the inception and prosecution of this unnatural war.

"The voice of the Council and Standing Committee, thus properly expressed, is to be regarded, first, as an earnest expression of opinion in a matter deeply concerning the welfare of the Diocese and the general good; and, secondly, as their united testimony to the continued and growing evil resulting from the omission referred to as practiced in one instance.

"Painfully conscious myself, as my brethren of the clergy and laity have thus been, of the unhappy effects of such nonconformity in so important a particular; and feeling that with the progress and developments of the war, the evil has increased rather than abated, I must confess my own thoughts for some time past had been turned to the propriety of the course here indicated. Under all the circumstances, therefore, my own deep convictions lead me to acquiesce in the wishes of those who are alike interested with me in all that relates to the welfare of the Church and the advancement, by every proper means, of the cause which we have so much at heart. The said permission will, therefore, be withdrawn in the only case in which it is now exercised—not to force the conscience of any one—God forbid!—but with the fervent prayer and earnest hope that it may lead to uniformity in our public devotions at least, and to the promotion of the spirit of unity and peace.

"Affectionately yours, in Christ,

"Houston, June 15, 1864.
"ALEXANDER GREGG,
"Bishop of Texas."

"Houston, June 23, 1864.

"DEAR BROTHER GILLETTE: I inclose you herewith copies of a pastoral which I have issued to the clergy, and which will explain itself. The permission granted to you heretofore to omit the words 'which has been forced upon us' in the first special prayer put forth by me is hereby withdrawn. I trust you may see your way open to a full conformity in this particular, and that this source of trouble and pain will no longer exist. Yours truly,

"ALEXANDER GREGG."

In the Pastoral, as given above, the Bishop uses this language: "The said permission will therefore be withdrawn in the only case in which it is now exercised—not to force the conscience of any one—God forbid!" This language will seem somewhat strange when I state that from the very first I had told him it was with me a matter of conscience not to use the words in question. He had been for three years in the habit, whenever present, of reading his prayer and relieving me. After publishing his Pastoral, he reached home about midnight, on Saturday night. He sent a servant early on Sunday morning to my house, to ask me to meet him at the vestry-room at nine o'clock. What could be the object of this hasty meeting? I did not even know he had returned— was it to tell me he sympathized with me, and would do all he could to relieve me? that he would still take the part of the service in which his prayer occurred, as he had done for three years? Oh! no; it was to tell me that he could no longer assist me. I must take all the service myself, and use the hitherto omitted words. Did he want to force my conscience, or what did he want?

So far as the public was concerned, I had remained silent up to the time of publishing the following letter in the Austin *State Gazette*. The action of the Convention, called forth by my course, and aimed at myself, had been before the public for two years, and there had been great misrepresentation, while I had not been heard. I felt therefore when the Bishop again brought the matter before the public through his Pastoral that I ought to try to be heard in turn. I understood the editor of the *Gazette* to promise that he would publish not only the following letter, but the entire correspondence, the next letter of which I told him was then ready on my part for publication. The Bishop had his reply published in the same number with my letter, and so great was his influence with the editor, that, although I understood him to have promised to continue to publish the correspondence, after talking with the Bishop, he refused to publish, even if I paid him for it at his advertising rates. So I was compelled to remain unheard.

CORRESPONDENCE

BETWEEN THE RT. REV. ALEX. GREGG, D.D., BISHOP OF THE DIOCESE OF TEXAS, AND THE REV. CHARLES GILLETTE, RECTOR OF ST. DAVID'S, AUSTIN.

"EDITOR STATE GAZETTE:

DEAR SIR: As you published the Pastoral Letter of Bishop Gregg, will you please insert the following reply? I sent a copy for publication to the *Galveston News*, in which several mistakes occur, and on this account I should much prefer a publication in your paper.

"Yours, truly, CHARLES GILLETTE.
"AUSTIN, July 30, 1864."

"MY DEAR BISHOP: I have received your Pastoral, and the accompanying note, withdrawing the permission granted to omit the words, 'which has been forced upon us,' in the first special prayer put forth by yourself for use during the present war. I can not, as you desire, 'see my way open to a full conformity' in the particular referred to, for reasons which I will proceed respectfully to state.

"I have for a long time acquiesced, in what now very plainly seems to me, a violation of canon law; and had not my attention been called more particularly to this matter, by your Pastoral, and the accompanying note, I might have continued quietly to transgress the law of the Church. But being forced to take a position before the public, I will endeavor to do so, in the fear of God, and in obedience to what I believe to be the law of the Church. This will compel me in future, in public worship, to omit the two special prayers put forth by yourself, and to use in the place of these, the prayer appointed by the Church, to be used 'In Time of War and Tumults.'

"The Constitution and Canons of the Church in the United States were adopted by our General Council, making only such changes as were necessary to adapt them to our civil government. The House of Bishops in their 'Pastoral Letter,' inform us of this identity, with the minor exceptions here referred to.

"By a reference to the 'Digest of Canons' put forth in 1860, you will observe, that Section 14 of Canon XIII., Title 1, (under the authority of which, the two special prayers now in use in this Diocese were put forth,) reads as follows: 'The Bishop of each Diocese may compose forms of prayer or thanksgiving, as the case may require, for extraordinary occasions, and transmit them to each Clergyman within his Diocese, whose duty it shall be to use such forms in his Church on such occasions.' You will also observe that Canon XX., Title 1, reads as follows: 'Every minister shall, before all sermons and lectures, and on all other occasions of public worship, use the Book of Common Prayer, as the same is or may be established by the authority of the General Convention of this Church; and in performing such service, no other prayers shall be used than 'those prescribed by the said Book.' The Eighth Article of the Constitution of the Church declares, that 'no alteration or addition shall be made in the Book of Common Prayer, or other offices of the Church or the Articles of Religion, unless the same shall be proposed in one General Convention, and by a resolve thereof made known to the Convention of every Diocese, and adopted at the subsequent General Convention. I believe that the Canon and Article here quoted contain all the law of the Church pertaining to the subject now under discussion.

"I think it is a general rule adopted in all courts, civil, criminal, ecclesiastical, or military, that the different parts or sections of a law must be so construed as to harmonize, where this is possible. In the present case, there seems to be no conflicting in the law. The Twentieth Canon makes it obligatory for all ministers to use the prayers prescribed in the Book of Common Prayer, *on all occasions of public worship, and no other prayers*. The Fourteenth Section of Canon XIII. makes an exception, and requires the Clergy of any Diocese to use the prayer or thanksgiving set forth by the Bishop for an 'extraordinary occasion,' which must mean a special service. There is then no conflicting in the Canons, and this point seems clearly established, namely, That the Church requires her clergy to use the prayers of the Book of Common Prayer on all occasions of public worship, and no other, with the single exception, that, on an 'extraordinary occasion' or special service, they must also use the prayer or thanksgiving set forth by the Bishop for that occasion.

"*Secondly.* I am not aware that 'extraordinary occasion' in the Fourteenth Section of Canon XIII. has been interpreted to mean any thing more than a single, special occasion, previous to the present war; no prayer having been put forth by any Bishop for continuous use in public worship previous to this time. This is further evident from the fact that the Church has composed, and set forth, a form of prayer to be used in cases where there is likely to arise a necessity for the continued use of such prayer. Therefore, it is evident she has given her Bishops no power to compose forms of prayer which shall be used on all occasions of public worship, year after year; as this would be in violation of the Eighth article of the Constitution of the Church, by changing the Liturgy, and to all intents and purposes, for the time being, the Book of Common Prayer.

"*Thirdly.* I conceive that where the Church has provided herself with a prayer for any occasion, and placed the same in the Book of Common Prayer, she has not granted to her Bishops permission to set such prayer aside, and to substitute one of their own in its place, or to add another prayer to hers, for the purpose of recording an 'historical fact' in connection with what may be deemed an 'extraordinary occasion' of long duration. But if 'extraordinary occasion' be interpreted to mean a continued season, during which public worship often recurs, even then her Clergy are bound to use the prayer set forth in the Book of Common Prayer, and no other. Who ever heard of a Bishop in the Church, issuing a prayer for the use of congregations, in time of 'Dearth and Famine,' or of 'Great Sickness and Mortality,' or during a 'Session of Congress,' whether ordinary or extraordinary? Why then should it be done in 'Time of War and Tumults?'

"*Fourthly.* It would be begging the question to say that a 'Time of War' was an 'extraordinary occasion' contemplated by the Canon. If this be so, the prayer provided by the Church becomes useless, and a nullity, and the Prayer-Book itself subject to any Bishop, during the continuance of war; and Bishops of different opinions, may introduce 'historical facts,' exactly contrary, and require the clergy and laity of the different Dioceses respectively to adopt them as matters of faith. By the same reasoning, any of the other occasions contemplated by the Church, and for which she has prepared special prayers, might be declared an 'extraordinary occasion,' for which a Bishop might prepare a special prayer, into which he might introduce, not only an 'historical fact,' but any false or corrupt doctrine, and make these also articles of faith. Can it be supposed that the Church has granted any such permission?

"*Fifthly.* The period these prayers have been in use; the universal consent of the Clergy, and the request of the Council, establish no prescriptive right. If the Canons have thus been unintentionally violated, it forms no reason why the infraction should be continued. Certainly a precedent against the Constitution and written law is not to be followed.

"*Sixthly*, While a clergyman is bound to obey his Bishop in lawful matters, yet (inasmuch as the Bishop is bound by the Constitution and Canons of the Church) he has no right to order any thing which contravenes these, and if he does, his Clergy are not bound to obey. Should an 'extraordinary occasion' arise, coming within the purview of the Canon, and for which the Church has not provided, and the Bishop should set forth a prayer or thanksgiving, to be used in the Diocese, I should be bound to use it on such occasion in obedience to his authority.

"I regret exceedingly, that, in regard to the public services of the Church, there should be any difference of opinion between my Bishop and myself. In regard to the use of the words 'which has been forced upon us,' it has been with me a matter of conscience from the beginning, as I informed my Bishop at the first, when he gave me permission to omit them. I have seen nothing to change my views upon this subject, and consequently I have the same conscientious scruples, now, that I have always had, and therefore could not use the words as they were intended. In carefully reviewing the Canons of the Church, I have come to a conclusion concerning the use of the two special prayers, not previously entertained, which satisfies my mind, that to use *any* special prayers set forth by a Bishop constantly in public worship, is a violation of the laws of the Church, and therefore I can not conscientiously continue to do this. The Church has prepared her own prayer for 'Time of War and Tumults,' which reads as follows: 'O Almighty God, the Supreme Governor of all things, whose power to create no creature is able to resist, to whom it belongeth justly to punish sinners, and to be merciful to those who truly repent; save and deliver us, we humbly beseech thee, from the hands of our enemies; that we being armed with thy defense, may be preserved evermore from all perils, to glorify thee who art the only giver of all victory: through the merits of thy Son Jesus Christ our Lord.'

"The Canon requires the clergy, if they use any prayer, *to use this* and *nò other.*

"There seems to have been a false impression made upon the public mind, from my not using the words, 'which has been forced upon us,' making this a sign of my hostility to the government. For this impression there has been no just cause. Had the words in question contained sentiments directly contrary to those expressed, I should still object to using them, as intending to assert a political fact, and on this account not admissible in a form of public prayer for constant use; being opposed to the spirit, if not the letter of the Canons; and to the usage of the Church. But the great question in my mind, is now, as it ever has been, one of *liberty of conscience*, and of *ecclesiastical law.*

"I think I know the duties of citizenship. These I intend faithfully to perform. But I do not intend to leave the performance of the sacred duties of my ministerial office, to mingle in the strife of *politics* or of *civil government* or of *war.* These things belong to others, but not to me. I can not suppose that I should further either my own salvation, or the salvation of others, by mixing in any such arena of strife. I regret that those around me are not willing that I should quietly attend to the sacred duties of my office. But whatever others may say or do, there is but one safe course for me to pursue, and that is to approve myself to God, and my own conscience. Yours truly,

CHARLES GILLETTE.

"Right Rev. ALEXANDER GREGG, D.D.,
July 2, 1864."

"AUSTIN, July 20, 1864.

"BROTHER GILLETTE: Your communication of the second instant, in reply to my note of the twenty-third ultimo, accompanying the Pastoral, was handed to me two days since, in which you inform me that, for the reasons therein stated, you will feel compelled in future, in public worship, not only to decline conformity as to the words 'which has been forced upon us,' but, further, to omit entirely the two special prayers put forth by me to be used during the present war.

"Were your reasons more satisfactory than they appear to me to be, I should yet much doubt the propriety in such a case, deeply affecting uniformity in our public worship and the consequent peace of the Church, in thus opposing in this seemingly insubordinate way your individual interpretation, not only to the course of this Diocese, but of the entire Church of the confederacy. Look *well* to it lest the plea of conscience, which has already been productive of so much disturbance and evil amongst us, and so greatly marred your usefulness, prove in the end an *ignis fatuus*, leading you into a bog from which there will be no extrication. It would be sad for you if the course you propose to pursue should be found but to add the guilt of contumacy to the grievous error, to say the least of it, with which your course for the past three years has been justly chargeable.

"Though your determination seems to be fixed, I pray that it may not be too late for reconsideration, and that even now you may be saved from such unhappy consequences and guided aright.   Yours truly,

"ALEXANDER GREGG.
"Rev. C. GILLETTE."

"AUSTIN, July 21, 1864.

"MY DEAR BISHOP: Your note acknowledging the receipt of mine of the second instant (which your absence from home prevented you from receiving earlier) is before me. I had hoped that if my reasoning did not satisfy your mind, you would have shown me its fallacy or have referred me to some other canon bearing upon the subject, and so have given me some ground for changing my position. In this I am altogether disappointed. Your language in regard to 'conscience' and 'contumacy' is very hard for me to comprehend. I think I understand the implied threat; still, I do not know that threats should move a man conscious of committing no offense. The grave charges you make against me are in my judgment utterly without foundation. A man who feels with all his soul that he is striving to fulfill his duty in the fear of God, ac-

cording to the holy Scripture and the law of the Church, can well commit his cause to the Almighty and leave results with Him.   Yours truly,
"C. GILLETTE.
"Rt. Rev. ALEXANDER GREGG."

In publishing the following letter, the Bishop, as he states in his note to the editor, made some considerable additions, thus making it to differ from the one he sent to me. I was not aware that in publishing a correspondence such things were done. He speaks of the time elapsing from the date of my letter until he received it, as if I had committed some great fault in this. I had already told him that the reason was his absence from home, and I did not know where a letter would reach him. He also complains of my publishing my letter when he saw it was in answer to his published Pastoral, sent to me as well as his note. I had been arraigned before the public, but I might not be heard there. How much cause there was for complaint, the public can now judge.

"AUSTIN, July 30, 1864.

"MR. RICHARDSON: It is unusual in this form to bring any matters of difficulty, connected with the Church, before the public. The appearance, however, in the *News Bulletin* of Wednesday last, of Rev. C. Gillette's communication to me, of the second instant, (received more than two weeks after that date,) makes it imperative on me, in justice both to the Church and myself, to depart in this instance from a rule so manifestly proper, by sending you my reply for publication. As to the circumstances which led to its being written, it will explain itself. It is not my wish or intention to engage in a public controversy—for having sent Mr. Gillette, in the first instance, a short, admonitory letter, I wrote at further length simply in compliance with his expressed wish and for his perusal, without any view whatever to publication, and with not the slightest intimation of such a design on his part; and now only desire to give another view of the important subject he brings out. There is not as much detail on some points as appearance in the public prints would seem to demand. I send it, however, as it is, with a few additions and changes, feeling assured, that under the circumstances, in the course here pursued, my motives will be appreciated.

"Yours truly, ALEXANDER GREGG."

"AUSTIN, July 22, 1864.

"BROTHER GILLETTE: Your note of yesterday is before me. After reading your communication of the second instant, setting forth your reasons at large for the course you propose to pursue, and stating, that being forced to do it, you had come to a conclusion and taken a position, I felt it would be useless to say any thing by way of reply to your argument, or of throwing light on the subject for your guidance. I was the more confirmed in this feeling by what I had heard of your course in St. David's, on the third instant—*a course*, unwarrantable, irregular, and well calculated, as it actually proved, to lead to the most serious results. It was, indeed, a finishing stroke at the unity of this unfortunate parish, aimed by yourself at the very vitals of its peace and spiritual welfare. I must speak plainly on *this*, as well as other points, which your note of yesterday makes proper, and which the occasion imperiously demands at my hands.

"In your last, you express disappointment that I did not attempt to show the fallacy of your reasoning, thus giving you some ground for changing your position. Therefore, notwithstanding my previous conviction that it would be useless, I will say something on the subject. But let me first remark, that you strangely misconstrue my words of warning into a *threat*. This would have been as unbecoming in me as beyond my province.

"As to the prescribed use of the Prayer-Book on occasions of public worship, and the mode of making any change therein, there can be no question. The simple point in the case is, does the Canon, authorizing a bishop to put forth Special Prayers, etc., justify the use of such special prayers as have been provided in this instance, both here and elsewhere in the Confederacy, as well as at the North? You think not; and, as I understand it, on two grounds chiefly: First, that 'extraordinary occasion,' as the words are used in the Canon, must mean a 'special service,' or a single 'special occasion,' and that no other interpretation has prevailed prior to the present war. Surely this reasoning, or assertion rather, is altogether specious. For why may not an occasion in effect and reality be *continuous*, not only for one or two or three services, or a few days or weeks, but even longer? How would you define it? As being confined to *one day*, or to one service? What authority or precedent is there for such a position? None whatever, since, prior to the present time, the question had never been raised. The *very fact*, that the Church herself has provided Special Prayers to be used during extraordinary occasions, or *circumstances*, if you prefer the latter term; or exigencies—as times of 'Dearth and Famine,' or 'War and Tumults'—these being always supposed to continue for a longer or shorter season, proves your whole position fallacious, showing, as it does, that even Special Prayers are provided for periods of indefinite duration. And why, on the same ground, may not such special prayers as those in question be likewise proper here? Point me to a single precedent, or interpretation, prior to your own, to the contrary! It is simply taken for granted by you, that 'extraordinary occasion' must mean a single, special occasion, or service. Whereas, in truth, the general precedent, both North and South, from the beginning of this great convulsion, is to the contrary—bishops prescribing, and clergy and laity acquiescing in the propriety, and even *necessity*, in view of the devotional wants of our people in such a crisis, of something of the kind. And is this nothing to make a man distrust his own view—to enforce obedience to lawful authority and to quiet his conscience, at least as to any responsibility of his in the matter? Many of those who have thus prescribed and acquiesced have had much to do with the framing of Canons, with their interpretation, and the practice of the Church in such matters. Is all this in no wise to influence a conscience, so delicately tender, as, at the very thought of a possible departure from the Canon, or, the acting where a doubt remains, to bleed at every pore? Again, I tell you, *beware* of *such a conscience*, with its plea of prayerful investigation, and (if it is opposed, or thought not to be justified in a certain course of conduct) its cry of persecution for righteousness' sake!

"But, your second ground of argument is to this effect, namely, that if 'extraordinary occasion' be interpreted to mean a continued season, during which public worship often occurs, even then her clergy are bound to use the prayers set forth in the 'Book of Common Prayer, and no other,' etc., as you state to be prescribed by Canon. This applies only to the regular ordinary service, for the bishops are authorized by Canon to put forth other prayers. This supposed interpretation and your reply to it, narrows down the issue very much to the point therein raised, and I call your special attention to what follows on the subject. Dr. Hawks, the highest authority as an expounder of our Constitution and Canons, in commenting on the Canon in question, uses these words; and you will observe particularly that he supposes the strongest case, because one in which a full and ample service is provided. His language is, and I quote it all:

"'One of the questions that may arise under this Canon, is this: Can the Bishop, when a service is set forth by the Church, in the Book of Common Prayer, make any additions to that service? Thus there is in the Prayer-Book, a form of prayer and thanksgiving, directed to be used yearly, on the first Thursday in November, or on such other day as shall be appointed by the civil authority. Has the Bishop authority to compose any additional prayer to be used in that service? Is any case an extraordinary occasion, within the meaning of the Canon, for which the Church has made provision? It may, indeed, be said that the thanks set forth in the Special Service, are for the fruits of the earth particularly, and that it seems fit to express our gratitude for other mercies also. Doubtless it is so, but the general thanksgiving of the Morning Service, is supposed to do that sufficiently, for it is directed to be used immediately before the Special Collect for the fruits of the earth, and the service is entitled 'a form,' etc., for the fruits of the earth, and *all the other blessings of His 'merciful Providence.'* The case of these other blessings, it would therefore seem, is, in the view of the Church, met by the general thanksgiving. Some of our bishops have taken a different view of the subject, and set forth a form additional for thanksgiving-day. The matter is of very little moment, however, except as involving a principle. Uniformity of liturgical worship, in the public services of the house of God, is the motto of churchmen; and, inasmuch as the bishops are not likely all to set forth the same form, this uniformity is lost. Wherever the Church has provided a service, we think it would be best not to deem the period appointed for its use an extraordinary occasion. The objection sometimes made, that the Bishop, by his own act, alters the Book of Common Prayer, in setting forth the form, is founded on a mistake. The Bishop has, indeed, no authority to *alter* the service, and he does not alter a word of it—he retains it all, but adds to it.'

"From all this we are to infer, that, in this distinguished writer's view, First, when a 'service' is provided, it would simply be *best* not to deem the period appointed for its use an extraordinary occasion; it not appearing, however, that he supposes a short, general prayer, to be synonymous with a service. Second, that an extraordinary occasion may be for a period. Third, that it is a matter of very little moment, except as involving the principle of liturgical uniformity. Fourth, that the right of a bishop to make the addition, if he sees proper to do so, is not questioned. Fifth, that such additions, even in the case of a full, special service, have been made and practiced—showing, as we may add, that had the canonical propriety of such a course been questioned, some subsequent General Convention would have amended the Canon so as to make it more explicit on the subject, or the House of Bishops would have expressed its opinion formally, to make the practice uniform if possible. Such being the case in these particulars, and with such authority and practice in view, what shall be thought of a clergyman, stepping forward and saying, I take a certain view of the Canon, and will not read the prayers put forth by my Bishop? Can you for a moment believe, that such a man as Dr. Hawks, writing as he does here, would dream of such a course of conduct?

"Your objection, that 'if bishops are authorized to put forth such prayers to be used during a long season, there would be no uniformity,' etc., applies with as much force in principle to prayers for a single occasion, for which, according to your admission, if it be extraordinary and no provision is made, there would be authority to provide. The further objection, that false doctrine or new articles of faith might thus be imposed upon the Church, is met by the simple fact, that such erroneous or false teaching would, in the mode appointed by the Church, at once receive due correction and punishment.

"In dwelling with so much emphasis upon the thought, that because certain Prayers are provided, as for a 'Time of War and Tumults,' no others are to be added, you entirely overlook the fact that such prayers may have been and doubtless were provided for very different reasons than to prevent others from being put forth and used—as, for example, simply to make some general and permanent provision for the use of the Church in case nothing else should be done. For the Bishops are not *required* to put forth such special Prayer for extraordinary occasions. The language of the Canon is, they *may*. But, the Bishop may see fit not to do so, or he may be absent, or there may be, for the time, no Bishop; in which cases, were no provision whatever made, a painful want would be experienced. But, consider the Prayer for a 'Time of War and Tumults.' It is short and very general. It does not meet the universal devotional wants of the people at such a time as this. It is admirably framed, indeed, as far as it goes, and you and every clergyman are at liberty to use it. But it manifestly falls short of what the heart now, in its approaches to God in public worship, longs to express more in detail; and hence, with singular unanimity, this general want has been provided for by additional special prayers.

"You remark, 'that she (the Church) has not granted permission to add another prayer to hers for the purpose of recording an historical fact.' Do you not know, for it has been explained to you again and again, that the words referred to here, as to an historical fact, were incidentally introduced into the prayer at the time it was composed, without any special thought, and only came under particular consideration when you asked permission to omit them? You are perfectly aware that *their insertion* was not the primary or secondary object of the prayer at all. Why then such an implied assertion? You further argue that other facts might be introduced, and so the privilege grossly abused. In reply, let me ask, is the sense of propriety and judgment of the Bishop in such cases not to be at all trusted?

"In closing, for I have written hurriedly and under the pressure of very limited time, I must add, that, in my view, you have taken a radically false position as to your responsibility in the matter of canonical obedience. And I do not hesitate to say, and charge you before God to bear it in mind, that you have not the *right* in such a case, (it being one not of flagrant wrong or palpable violation,) where the general language of the Canon, for it is of necessity general, authorizes the Bishop to put forth prayers, as in the case before us, and especially where, as here, there is no precedent to the contrary, but rather a general acquiescence and practice—that you have not *the right* to raise the question and make the issue of canonical interpretation in the way you propose, by an act of positive disobedience to lawful authority—therein setting an example, always pernicious, of open insubordination in the Church of God. The Church herself has provided by Canon and custom alike, how such errors (if indeed it be an error on the part of your Bishop in this case) are to be corrected, namely, by an amendatory Canon, or an expression of opinion, hitherto deemed to a certain extent authoritative, by the House of Bishops. Even the citizen is bound to obey the law, though he thinks it unjust or unconstitutional, until a competent tribunal has decided the question. The member of the Church is bound to reverence her teaching and obey her voice, clearly ascertained and plainly enforced, until, should their correctness be questioned, some authoritative decision is pronounced, as by a General Council. And so, here, until a legitimate and authoritative expression on the subject shall be obtained, it is the bounden duty of every clergyman within the pale of the Church to *conform*. Should he set authority at defiance, as you propose to do, and persist in his opposition, such a course can only be deemed unchurch-like, irreverent, insubordinate and contumacious in its essential character and tendencies; for what is your ordination vow, but that you 'will reverently obey your Bishop, following, with a glad mind and will, his godly admonition, and submitting yourself to his godly judgment'?

"Furthermore, you will permit me to say, that it would have been better for you and your troubled conscience, had you looked more carefully than you appear to have done into the nature and limits of human responsibility. A misguided conscience, for example, in this matter of responsibility as to our peculiar institution, was one of the most active causes at work in *forcing* this war upon us. Suppose it to be the case, that there is some ground for questioning the canonical propriety of Special Prayers like those in use here for a 'Time of War'—that the subject is at least involved in doubt—*you* are not responsible in the case at all. The Bishop has to bear that; and no one would imagine, that should he have erred in judgment, any guilt in such a case would be incurred. Leave the responsibility with him. Let the point be decided, if need be, in the *right way* and at the *right time*, and 'study to do your own business.' I *repeat it*—under the Canon, this question of interpretation here is not for you to decide. You should not trouble yourself with the matter. It is properly left in other hands. Your duty is in another line of action, namely, that of canonical obedience and conformity. The spirit of meekness at least should dictate such a course of conduct. So much for the omission of the prayers *in toto*, as you propose, which you have now made the plea for non-conformity, shifting from your original position of merely omitting the words, 'which has been forced upon us.'

"Going back to the omission of these words, let me remark, that the only proper course for you to pursue, should your conscience absolutely forbid their use, is to resign your position, and not force a painful and distracting issue upon the Church. You are not bound to remain where you are, under such circumstances, the permission having been withdrawn. And I put it to your conscience, whether it would not be better for the peace of the Church, and the spiritual welfare of her members, as well as for all parties concerned, that you should quietly withdraw, rather than take a step, which will inevitably make the state of things worse than it has been, and tend to serious and manifold evil?

"You remark, as you have done on other occasions, that you 'do not intend to leave the performance of the sacred duties of your ministerial office to mingle in the strife of politics, or of civil government, or of war. These things belong to others, but not to me. I can not suppose that I should further either my own salvation, or the salvation of others, by mixing in any such arena of strife.' This I understand to be an implied insinuation, that there are *others* who do all this. Now let me tell you, that if there are any of our brethren chargeable with such a course, I do not know them; and furthermore, let me say in all candor, that they are just as earnestly intent on discharging the duties of their sacred calling, and as laboriously engaged in forwarding the salvation of others, as yourself. In my opinion, as in that of most of our people, you have really taken as decided a position and been as active in exerting a *certain influence* in connection with the war, as any other. *Nay*, that you are justly chargeable with having brought on the unhappy state of things in this matter, that now exists in the Church.

"You seem to think, that the action of your Bishop and of the Council has been aimed at yourself personally, and the only endeavor made, *that* to force your conscience! This is far, *very far*, from the truth. It has only been to restore uniformity, peace, and quiet. Your *position*, unhappily taken at the outset and persisted in, has been the fruitful source of the evil. Not *alone* the omission of the words, 'which has been forced upon us,' as you seem to imagine, but many other things also have induced the public to think, that your *real, deepest sympathies*, as a man and a minister, have not been with us in this perilous struggle. And let me tell you, once for all, *that* impression *never will* be, *never can* be effaced. I leave you, in the matters involved, to God and your conscience. Yours truly,
"ALEXANDER GREGG.
"Rev. C. GILLETTE."

"AUSTIN, July 23, 1864.

"MY DEAR BISHOP: Your communication, handed me last evening, contains the opinion of Dr. Hawks upon the 14th Section of Canon XII., Title 1, and your deductions therefrom, which requires further consideration by me. I had expected to open my church for divine service to-morrow, in accordance with my intention announced in my communication of the second instant. I do not wish to act hastily, but rather to arrive at truth. I will therefore delay opening the church to-morrow, and will thank you to loan me the work of Dr. Hawks for a day or two, as I desire to examine several points not referred to in your communication. I had before desired to refer to the work of this distinguished canonist, but did not know that a copy could be had in town.

"Yours truly,   C. GILLETTE.

"Rt. Rev. ALEX'R GREGG."

"AUSTIN, July 23, 1864.

"BROTHER GILLETTE: I have been out this morning until a few moments since. Your note is before me. As you desire further time for consideration, and propose not to open the church to-morrow, I write to ask whether, under the circumstances, it would not be better for me to officiate in the church. I will cheerfully do so, and make the offer chiefly on account of the congregation, which has been two Sundays without service. As there is thus no necessity for it, it seems to me they should not be deprived of service to-morrow.

"I send Dr. Hawks's work.

"Yours truly,   ALEX. GREGG.

"Rev. C. GILLETTE."

NOTE.—In the preceding letter, the Bishop seems very anxious the congregation should have service. He did not wish "to force any man's conscience." Why could he not have done as he had been doing for two years previous, whenever he was present in the church, namely, assist the Rector, and take that portion of the service in which his unfortunate prayer occurred? Such a course might have relieved, for a season, at least, the Rector, whom he knew to be surrounded by bayonets and threatened with a halter. It would have allayed public clamor; but it would not have made the Rector cease to officiate, nor have driven him from the Diocese.

"GOVALLEY, July 24, 1864.

"MY DEAR BISHOP: I was in the country yesterday, and did not receive your note until about dark. I should be glad for you to have service to-day, as you propose. Please inform me by the bearer, that I may know what to do in regard to ringing the bell. Yours truly,
"Rt. Rev. ALEX. GREGG. C. GILLETTE."

NOTE.—To the above the Bishop returned a verbal answer, that he desired not to officiate. The following Saturday he addressed the following note to the Rector:

"Will Brother Gillette inform me what he purposes to do, so far, at least, as to enable me to know what to expect, as to service to-morrow?"
"July 30, 1864. ALEX. GREGG."

"GOVALLEY, July 30, 1864.
"MY DEAR BISHOP: I have been suffering most of this week from a slight bilious attack, occasioned, as I think, by too much exposure to the hot sun, and so have not as yet completed my answer to yours of the twenty-second instant. I shall not have service in St. David's to-morrow, but, if you desire, will open the church for you.
"Yours truly, CHARLES GILLETTE.
"Rt. Rev. ALEX. GREGG."

"BROTHER GILLETTE: I am sorry to hear of your indisposition. Will officiate (D.V.) as you propose to-morrow, and give notice accordingly. ALEX. GREGG.
"July 30, 1864."

For the better understanding of the reader, I will here state, that the act so strongly condemned by the Bishop, as having taken place on the third of July, was simply this: It was the first Sunday in the month, and I had given notice for the communion; but in the mean time I had received the Bishop's Pastoral and note, withdrawing the permission to omit the words. I could not use them. If I proceeded as usual on that Sunday, and omitted them, I knew that would create excitement. I therefore concluded simply to have the communion service and communion, and dismiss the congregation, which I did. This the Bishop pronounces " *a course* unwarrantable, irregular, and well calculated, as it actually proved, to lead to the most serious results." What there was so "unwarrantable" and "irregular" in all this, I do not understand. It is no uncommon thing to have the communion service with the communion by itself. I do not, therefore, see the necessity for the language used by the Bishop.

"MY DEAR BISHOP: A slight indisposition last week has prevented my returning as early an answer to your communication of the twenty-second ultimo as I intended. Before entering upon the argument connected with our subject, I must allude to some points in your letter, which require some notice in passing. In regard to what you say of what transpired in St. David's on the third of July, I reply, that what I did was done with the hope of allaying excitement, in performing, as far as possible, the duties devolving upon me on that day; and I can not suppose that the censure you apply is at all deserved. So, too, in regard to the censures and personalities contained in several parts of your communication, I must say, I think them unjust and out of place.

"Your remarks in regard to conscience, and your statements, either direct or implied, that mine is defective, may or may not be true. As you have in no way enlightened me, as to wherein it is defective, I remain as before, thinking it right. But even supposing it wrong, I had not expected a Bishop to ridicule or use sarcasm to correct a misguided conscience.

"I remember an eloquent divine to have said, that 'conscience is the voice of God in man;' and to me, as the faculty which decides what is right or wrong in action, it has seemed a something almost divine. I was not prepared, therefore, for a teacher of our holy religion to use such means as you seem to be using, to correct a too tender or misguided conscience. I am aware that a misguided conscience has led to manifold evils in the past, and will probably do so in the future. But still, I suppose every man must be his own judge of his conscientious convictions of duty; of course, doing what he can to exercise an enlightened conscience. In the case before me I have tried to do this, acting in the fear of God.

"You say: 'You have taken a radically false position, as to

your responsibility in the matter of canonical obedience. And I do not hesitate to say, and charge you before God, to bear it in mind, you have no right,' etc. And, again: 'Furthermore, you will permit me to say that it would have been better for you and your troubled conscience, had you looked more carefully than you appear to have done into the nature and limits of human responsibility.' Again: 'You are not responsible in the case at all, the Bishop has to bear that.' If I understand this kind of reasoning, it is, that a bishop is the law to his clergy, and if they break the plain law of the Church at his command, *he* is to blame, and not they. I do not think the Church, or Christianity, or good morals, teach any such doctrine as this. Although I have been trained from an early period of my life in the doctrines of the Church, yet I have never learned any such doctrine of 'human responsibility.' I believe that doctrine to be a prominent teaching of the Jesuits of the Church of Rome, but one which all Protestants utterly abjure. Look at it in the present case. I bound myself by a solemn obligation, amounting almost to an oath, when I was ordained, to obey the laws of the Church in conducting public worship. Those laws require me to use certain prayers, *and no others.* My Bishop tells me to disregard my solemn promise, and disobey the laws, and he will take all the responsibility, and free me. 'I do not understand any such mode of shifting responsibility, nor did I ever expect to hear it advocated by a Protestant clergyman. In another place you exhort me to obedience to the laws of the Church. To be obedient is what I am asking to be allowed. I desire to do as the Constitution and Canons require. If we could all return at once to be guided by these, there would no longer be any difficulty.

"Your strong reason for withdrawing the liberty hitherto granted, of omitting six words in your first payer, is based upon the plea of *uniformity.* Yet, you now tell me that I am at liberty to use the additional prayer from the Prayer-Book, which neither you nor the clergy of the diocese use. If I were to do this, how much would it further uniformity?

"Let us now turn to what may more properly be termed your argument in connection with the language of Dr. Hawks, and your deductions therefrom, as you seem to lay upon this language such stress. Permit me, however, to remind you that you seem entirely to overlook the positive language of the Twentieth Canon, and also of the Eighth Article of the Constitution, under which the present case falls; while the case referred to by Dr. Hawks might be said to fall under the Fourteenth Section of Canon Thirteen. He refers to a case which can occur at most but once a year, and always on Thursday, and so would not occur in the great majority of cases, on any occasion of public worship, and therefore might well be considered as an 'extraordinary occasion,' while the present case covers 'all occasions of public worship.' That service of once a year, Dr. Hawks gives it as *his* opinion, as best not to consider it an 'extraordinary occasion;' and, hence, that a bishop should not put forth a prayer, or thanksgiving for that occasion. Would not this distinguished canonist be somewhat astonished to find a Bishop so misconstruing his language—which expressly declares that in his judgment there is not ground for putting forth any addition to that yearly service—that he should plead from it the right to put forth prayers to be used on all occasions of public worship for a series of years,—and this, too, contrary to the express language of the Eighth Article of the Constitution, and also of the Twentieth Canon? It is impossible for me, and I think it would be for most men, to comprehend the assumption of analogy in the two cases, which would furnish a foundation for such deductions as are made. Let us look at them more in detail. Dr. Hawks is considering an occasion for a special service, happening once a year, and considered by *some* of the bishops as an 'extraordinary occasion,' and so coming under the exception provided for when they have a right to set forth an addition to the service prescribed. *His* opinion is against the custom of *some* bishops, and so would be opposed to you, even if the cases were analogous. The stress you lay on *service* loses its force, since the Church has provided a *service* for all *occasions*, whether ordinary or extraordinary. And the permission granted to a bishop is not to set forth a *service*, but simply a *prayer* or *thanksgiving*. Your second deduction, that an 'extraordinary occasion' may be a period, does not appear. The service set forth is for one day in each year, it is true, and that day specified, and so might be called an 'extraordinary occasion,' for one day in each year. But by what mode of reasoning this makes that day a period, or its annual recurrence a period, in the sense of which we are speaking, I can not understand; or how this example, recurring once a year, can be made to cover 'all occasions of public worship,' for a series of years, contrary to the express words of the Canon, and of the Constitution, is not evident to me; nor do I think it will be apparent to others. Your third deduction places Dr. Hawks entirely with me. He is speaking of uniformity in the whole Church, by using the Church's prayer, in opposition to uniformity being broken, by each bishop's putting forth his own prayer, even for that one occasion, and thus making each diocese the boundary of uniformity.

"Your fourth deduction, as to the right of a Bishop in the case mentioned, not being questioned, and your fifth, that neither the General Convocation nor the House of Bishops have done any thing to render the Canon more explicit, simply shows, that this service for one day in each year *may* be considered as an 'extraordinary occasion,' and the Church, with her usual modesty and kindness, leaves some liberty to her Bishops here, as to her clergy and laity elsewhere, although her uniformity may be broken by it. As, for instance, in the Creed, where she allows 'any churches' to omit altogether the words, 'He descended into hell,' or to substitute for them: 'He went into the place of departed spirits.'* What you say in your fifth deduction in regard to a *full service* is answered, as before, by the fact that the Church has just as much a *full service* for every Sunday and every day in the year as for the first Thursday in November, and indeed more so; for in her ritual for constant use she allows no change or addition, while for Thanksgiving day some think she allows

---

* I resided for several years in the Diocese of Virginia, and I know that in that diocese several congregations always. omitted the words in question, or made the substitution as permitted by the Church. The same is also done in other dioceses, and yet no one ever dreamed of its breaking uniformity, or disturbing the 'unity and peace' of the Church.

the addition as being an 'extraordinary occasion.' The language of our distinguished canonist, as quoted by you, is certainly very strong and very much to the point, namely: 'Wherever the Church has provided a service, we think it would be best not to deem the period appointed for its use an extraordinary occasion.' Such language is very decisive as to the author's opinion; and if he would say this in regard to a service occurring once a year, what would he say concerning the daily or weekly services—that is, services, in the language of the canon, for 'all occasions of public worship'? The Church has provided her *service* for 'Time of War and Tumults,' by furnishing a prayer to be used on all occasions of public worship during the continuance of war and tumults.

"But the real question is in regard to the language of the two Canons and the Eighth Article of the Constitution. The canons ought to be so construed as both to stand; and, as I stated in my former communication, I think this can easily be done. But if this can not be done, which Canon must take precedence? Evidently, the one regulating 'all occasions of public worship,' as the section defining what may be done on 'extraordinary occasions' is simply directing as to an exceptional case. This, I think, would be granted by all expounders of law, and hence the clergy would be bound by the Canon regulating *all clergymen* on *all occasions of public worship*, and so be required to use the 'prayers in the Book of Common Prayer, and *no others*.' But, again, our distinguished canonist decides, that although a Bishop does not *alter* the Book of Common Prayer, he adds thereto by his prayer or thanksgiving, (this must certainly be the case, if it is in constant use year after year,) which makes your prayers violate the Eighth Article of the Constitution, which declares that 'no alteration or *addition* shall be made to the Book of Common Prayer,' etc. The Constitution, if it can not be made to harmonize with the Canons, is the higher authority, and must take precedence. Every clergyman, before he is ordained, takes a solemn obligation to conform, not only to the doctrines, but to the worship of the Protestant Episcopal Church; and in addition to this, every Bishop, before he is consecrated, makes this solemn promise: 'In the name of God, amen: I, chosen Bishop of the Protestant Episcopal Church in ——, do promise conformity and obedience to the doctrine, discipline, and *worship* of the Protestant Episcopal Church in ——. So help me God, through Jesus Christ.'

"With these things before me, I do not see how a clergyman can use, or a Bishop enforce, the use of the prayers in question. That men may err when they do not know the law, is readily understood; but how ministers and Bishops can persist in a palpable violation of the Constitution and of plain law when they do know, is to me past comprehension.

"Your language in regard to the permissive character of the Canon, and your deduction therefrom in regard to the provision of special prayers in the Prayer-Book, seems without force, since the Canon itself goes on to make the very provision to satisfy your proposed case, stating that 'the clergy in those States or dioceses, or other places within the bounds of this Church, in which there is no Bishop, may use the form of prayer or thanksgiving composed by the Bishop of any diocese.' But there is a thought of much greater moment, concerning the permissive character of the language, which seems to have escaped your notice.

"Contrast the language of the Twentieth Canon and the Eighth Article of the Constitution with that of the fourteenth section of Canon Thirteenth, 'The Bishop of each diocese *may*,' fourteenth section of Canon Thirteenth; 'every minister *shall*,' Canon Twentieth; 'no alteration or *addition shall* be made,' Article Eighth. Yet the two *permissive* prayers under '*may*' are now made to violate the positive language '*shall*' of the Twentieth Canon and of the Eighth Article of the Constitution. There is another point in connection with the last provision of the Fourteenth section of Canon Thirteenth, which you seem to me to overlook, but which plainly limits the first part of the section, namely: 'Bishops *may* also compose forms of prayer to be used before legislative and other public bodies.' Would this permission allow a Bishop to introduce a prayer composed under it into the Church on '*all occasions of public worship*'? This would not be contended. Then why contend for it under the first permission? You say in regard to the prayer in the Prayer-

Book for 'Time of War and Tumults,' that 'it does not meet the universal devotional wants of the people at such a time as this.' This is the same argument, and almost the same language, used by those who for years have disturbed the peace of the Church by claiming that they were too straitened in the prayers of the Church; that more fullness and particularity were necessary in public worship, to meet present circumstances and passing events; and therefore latitude must be given for extemporaneous prayers. Is expediency to override the Constitution and the law? The Church does not seek to meet the wants of which you speak, in her *public services*. She inserts no 'historical facts,' as 'primary,' 'secondary,' or any other object of prayer. All her prayers are formed on a different model, and she wisely leaves the 'universal, devotional wants' to which you allude, to the social circle, the family, or the closet; and it is this very thing which, when rightly considered, will be perceived to form one of her strongest bonds of union and one of her mightiest towers of strength. She meets, in a general way, the spiritual wants of all, in language to which none can object; she intrudes individual opinion upon none, as a nucleus for contention and strife.

"You speak of precedent, and desire me to show it for my interpretation of the canons. You must certainly know that the usage or precedent of the Church up to the commencement of the present war, has been to consider 'extraordinary occasion' as a single service, or for one day only. It is easy to see how, in the general excitement incident to the present unhappy war, all might have readily fallen into the error of which we are speaking, but which is nevertheless a violation both of the Constitution and of the Twentieth Canon. I may here repeat, in substance, a remark made in my former communication. The period these prayers have been in use, the universal consent of the clergy, etc., form no prescriptive right. If the Canons have been unintentionally violated, this forms no reason why the infraction should be continued. I have alluded to these things briefly, lest you might suppose if I passed them by in silence, that they contained argument applicable to the present case. But the real argument in the case must rest on the language of the two Canons and the

Article of the Constitution. Can the two Canons and the Eighth Article be made to harmonize? If so, 'extraordinary occasion' does not cover all occasions of public worship, and so violates the express language of the Twentieth Canon and of the Eighth Article of the Constitution. If the two Canons do not harmonize, which is the ruling canon? Evidently the Twentieth, which is the general rule, rather than the Fourteenth Section of Canon Thirteenth, which is only the exception. But if the Canons and the Constitution disagree, which takes precedence? Evidently the Constitution is the higher authority; therefore it must stand, if the Canons fall. According to it, no *addition* must be made to the Book of Common Prayer. But there is perfect harmony between the Twentieth Canon and the Eighth Article of the Constitution, and as *either* of these would govern the Fourteenth Section of Canon Thirteenth, both together must settle the question beyond a doubt. As you seem so strangely determined on my violating the Constitution and law of the Church, urging as a reason your opinion as to the necessity or the expediency of the case, and the act of the Bishop in setting forth prayers, it may be quite pertinent to refer you to a short sentence of Dr. Hawks, bearing upon this subject. Says he: 'It seems to have been forgotten *that the usage of regulating the exercise of a Bishop's functions by certain fixed rules, is as ancient as the office of a Bishop.* There is as much of venerable antiquity in the custom of making laws for Bishops, as there is in making Bishops themselves. It may safely be affirmed that, since the days of the Apostles, they never were left with no guide but their own discretion.' I may add that your assumption that it is of no consequence to me if I violate the Constitution and laws of the Church, if I only obey your order or direction, seems to me to destroy these great truths lying at the foundation of all law, civil and ecclesiastical. The first is that no officer or citizen possesses any arbitrary power. The second, that, in the language of the greatest expounder of the common law, (the rules of which our canons make binding,) 'Law is the rule of civil conduct, presented by the superior power in the state;' or, as civilians say, 'It is a solemn expression of legislative will.' In the Church, our General Council, as the highest legislative body of the Church, has spoken. No Bishop can give an order for which he finds no authority in the law of the Church. An order which violates the Constitution and canons of the Church can not be conscientiously obeyed.

"It is a failure to observe these cardinal principles of self-preservation which has led to that 'higher-lawism' which has involved the country in the present terrible revolution. The argument of necessity, and the power of will and force, is daily destroying all the restraints of law. It seems to me, then, that you must recognize this truth, that precedents which violate the Constitution and law of the Church can never be invoked in the face of the written law.

"Yours truly, CHARLES GILLETTE.

"Right Rev. ALEXANDER GREGG, D.D.

"AUSTIN, August 2, 1864."

"AUSTIN, August 4, 1864.

"BRO. GILLETTE: I infer from your communication of the second, received yesterday afternoon, (and which will be answered in due time,) that you purpose to carry out your first intention of holding service, and omitting the two special prayers. I am well aware that a large part of the congregation, such is the state of feeling, will not attend your service; and, as you state in your last you desired by your course in church, on the third ultimo, to allay excitement, the question arises here, can no provision be made for those who will otherwise be without service, and no step taken to prevent more serious disturbance in the Church? I am willing to hold a separate service, and much prefer doing so, in the existing state of things; but do not wish, even in appearance, to act discourteously, or to seem to trample upon what might be considered the right of others, and therefore write at the outset, to know if you assent. I am satisfied the course I propose will be a great relief to many, and be attended with happy results. Please let me hear from you at your earliest convenience. Yours truly, ALEX. GREGG.

"Rev. C. GILLETTE."

"Austin, August 5, 1864.

"My Dear Bishop: Your communication of yesterday was handed me just at dark. In reply I would say, unless you can refer me to some further law upon the subject, I conceive the Constitution and the Canons would fully sustain me in pursuing the course indicated, but as you propose to answer me, I am willing to wait for further light, and for the sake of peace, to forego the exercise of a plain canonical right, and so for the present will invite you to have service and preach in St. David's. If this proposition is met by you with the spirit in which it is made, it will tend, in my judgment, much more to harmony and peace than any other course which is likely to be pursued. Yours, truly, Charles Gillette.
"Rt. Rev. Alex. Gregg."

Note.—To the above I had added the following: "Your proposition to divide the congregation makes it proper that I should here allude to some facts in the past. I was warned by a gentleman, now nearly two years since, after he had listened to some remarks of yours concerning this parish, that you would make an effort to divide it. I did not at the time think his remarks just, but I soon discovered what led me to fear he might have been correct in his deductions, made from your language. I intimated to you, not many months after, that, whether intended or not, you were exciting discord and contention in my parish. For a little season you were more guarded; but it was not long before your efforts, whether designed or not, became very apparent to myself, and others in the congregation. They have continued until you have made the proposition in writing to divide the parish. I have been satisfied for a long time that you had fully determined on one of two things, either to drive me from my parish, or to divide it. Although you have charged me as being responsible for the present state of feeling and division in this parish, yet there is a difference of opinion prevailing on that subject, as I and many others think that upon yourself rests the responsibility for the present unhappy state of things in St. David's. For more than two years you have not ceased to perform ministerial acts in my parish, in violation of the law of the Church, without consulting me, or asking my permission, (which of course would have been granted, if asked.)"

Just as I was about to send the foregoing, as a part of the last letter, three of my vestrymen called at my house, and informed me that a member of the congregation, just returned from the war, had taken it upon himself to circulate a paper, throwing the blame of the existing state of affairs in the parish upon the rector, and asking for signatures requesting him to resign. This individual was told the statement in regard to myself was not true, and he was advised to desist from any further efforts. He had gotten his own and two other signatures. The vestrymen advised me to leave off that portion of the letter above indicated, since, however true it might be, it would arouse ill-feeling. I followed their advice, and did not send it, but it is thought proper to insert it in publishing the correspondence.

"AUSTIN, August 5, 1864.

"BRO. GILLETTE: Yours of this morning has just been handed to me. I trust your proposition is met in the spirit with which it is made, as my only object and sincere desire is to do what may promote the Church's welfare, in accordance with the spirit and letter of her laws. I will, therefore, 'for the present,' (D. V.,) in compliance with your invitation, hold service and preach in St. David's, and doubt not, until your final action is taken, it will tend to peace.

"Yours truly, ALEX. GREGG.
"Rev. C. GILLETTE."

"AUSTIN, August 9, 1864.

"BRO. GILLETTE: I do not wish to protract this correspondence, especially as your last, of the second instant, shows very plainly that it has already reached a point, which will make it productive of no good result, but rather of evil. You only reiterate in a diluted form your first argument, and narrow down the issue, according to your own admission, to the interpretation of the Eighth Article of the Constitution and Twentieth Canon, in connection with Section Fourteen of Canon Thirteen, making it turn chiefly upon the former, and, if needs be, the first. While admitting the correctness of the general principle of interpretation you lay down, I must insist, as a *clear* and *indisputable point*, that the Eighth Article and Twentieth Canon have in reality nothing to do with the matter. The first forbids *any change* in the Book of Common Prayer, except in the mode prescribed. But who before yourself ever imagined that the use of certain special prayers for a time, though protracted, as in this instance, makes any change in the Prayer-Book? They form no part of that book in fact, were not intended to do so, and can not by any process of reasoning whatever be made to have such an effect. They are distinct from it, and so universally understood to be, simply being used in connection with it; though the extraordinary occasion of their use be protracted, they yet form a *temporary* and not a *permanent provision*. They were not put forth by the Bishop as *such*, and form no more a part of the Prayer-Book proper, than they do of the building in which they are read. The pastoral letters by which they were accompanied limited their use to *the war*. They are under no circumstances to go beyond it, and therefore, for the time being only, assume the character of special prayers put forth by a bishop. On the other hand, were the council of a diocese to issue certain prayers for general and permanent use, or were the general council, by its own action alone, and without submitting it to the dioceses, to prepare any thing of the kind, they would form an integral part of the Liturgy, and the Eighth Article might well be adduced to prove such action unconstitutional. But to apply it here, where no one dreamed that such a thing is done, and it is not so intended, is simply absurd; and a thousand pages of argumentation, could they be written, so plain it seems to me is the proposition, could not make it appear more so than it is.

"In like manner, the Twentieth Canon, which requires the use of the prayers in the Book of Common Prayer, and *no others*, does not apply here, as it would to the case of a clergyman, for example, using additional prayers of any sort of his own accord, without authority, or of a bishop doing the same. In fact, it does not apply in this case at all, and can not be made to do so. For here the Bishop acts expressly under the Canon, which provides for special prayers, and the only question that can possibly arise, is, does the Canon authorize such prayers as have been put forth here? This is a question, first, of interpretation, upon which we differ diametrically; and, second, of practice, as to which all the Church, bishops, clergy, and laity, except yourself, and perhaps a few others, are agreed. There is no previous precedent to fall back upon; and as not only a large majority, but the whole American Church, may be said to be of one mind, should it not settle the matter, at least, for the present? It must do so with all right-minded men of orderly spirit.

"I can not see, indeed, how any one under such circumstances, with, I may say, the whole Church against him, in a mere point of interpretation, and whose compliance on his part is made *imperative*, how he can resolve it into such a grave question of conscience! Is universal practice not to bear upon the decision of such a point? Is a man to stand out, and set *all authority* at defiance? How, then, are disputes, or controversies, ever to be ended? To what is such a spirit ever to yield? And when shall principles ever be settled, if usage, *universal usage*, is to have no weight? Such is the compass of the argument as you have narrowed it down, and, except incidentally, I will not dwell upon it further.

"My deductions from Dr. Hawks's language, presented without any argument, do not appear to me to be at all shaken by your comments thereon. And even if they were, it would only bear collaterally upon the question. Take, for instance, one of these deductions, the second, which affirms that 'extraordinary' occasion may be for a period, and does it not plainly and unanswerably follow from such language as this? 'Where the Church has provided a service, we think it would be best not to deem the period appointed for its use an extraordinary occasion.' Now, in the name of logic, what does this mean, if not, in Dr. Hawks's view, that where no service is provided, an extraordinary occasion may be for a period? The other point whether a *single prayer* is a *service*, in the sense here intended, is another question. But why argue such points? Is not their simple presentation decisive?

"You reason, that since the permission to a bishop to compose prayers to be used before legislative or other bodies, does not authorize their use on all occasions of public worship—no more should the permission to put forth special prayers for extraordinary occasions authorize any thing of the kind. This reasoning is remarkable indeed, and such a *non sequitur* as scarcely ever fell under my notice before! While pondering this permission to put forth prayers to be used before legislative bodies, etc., did it not occur to you that the prayer for Congress, with the prescribed change of a few words, would have answered quite as well, or better, according to your reasoning, than any such additional forms; and that the fact of its not being thus prescribed argues inferentially in favor of the authority to use other prayers for a time of war? And, further, did you not stop to ask yourself in another connection, if special prayers for extraordinary occasions are to be confined to one day, or one service, and not to be used for a continuous season, what the provision for the use of such prayers in a diocese where there was no bishop would have availed in the days when railroads were not so common, and communication was by no means speedy? As is not unfrequently the case, the bishop has scarcely time to publish them in his own diocese, what, then, would have become in other days of those outside? Does not the very fact of such a provision, therefore, imply that in the view of the framers of the Canon, it was deemed that an extraordinary occasion might be continuous?

"It is a gross and very extraordinary perversion of what I said as to *your responsibility* in this matter, to change it as you do in words like these: 'Those laws (of the Church) require me to use certain prayers and no others. My Bishop tells me to disregard my solemn promise and disobey the laws, and he will take all the responsibility and free me.' This sounds more like the incoherence of a man dreaming, than any thing else. Your Bishop told you no such thing. He meant nothing of the kind, and you should have known it. What he meant and plainly expressed was, that the Canon made *him*, in the first instance, responsible rather than yourself. Can you not take this idea in?

"With what holy horror you must have awoke to find your Bishop a Jesuit! And then again, by a sudden metamorphosis, to behold him contending for more latitude, as in the way of extempore prayer, etc., in the Church—first hurrying him rapidly forward on the road to Rome, and then to Geneva! Can you not settle his real *status* a little better than that?

"How simple a fact it is under the Canons, that certain of them throw responsibility directly on the Bishop, others on the clergyman, others on both—that is all! No, no! Accuse me not of being willing to shoulder your *responsibility* in this matter. I should certainly stagger and fall by the wayside under the burden! It is enough for me, God knows, to endeavor to meet my own.

"You kindly send your Bishop his solemn consecration vow, as though it were not familiar to him; and then, after some remarks, indulge in this language, (what shall I say in describing it?) 'How ministers and bishops can persist in a palpable violation of the Constitution and of plain law, when they do know it, is to me past comprehension.' And well it may be! Did you weigh these words? Do you now fully comprehend their import? Did your conscience whisper nothing while you were penning such a grave reflection upon the ministers and bishops of the Church? But to complete the lesson, you quote, for my edification, Dr. Hawks's language as to laws having been made for Bishops as well as others, and their being bound by these laws. Will you pardon me for saying, that I read this passage nearly twenty years since? Have I ever uttered a word to the contrary? Take care lest, in the zeal of a late conversion to the truth in the interpretation of our Constitution and Canons, you go beyond yourself, and become a 'new light,' and the foremost canonical reformer of the age; for you may find yourself, like many others have done, breaking down in the race!

"I had intended saying a word or two as to the singular means you charge me with using, in dealing with too tender a conscience. Did I really say it was too tender? As I thought I understood the disease, was not the remedy rightly left to my own choosing? What you deem personalities were only a legitimate reply, in truth, to remarks which you had made, and were so intended. But enough of this, as of my reply in general to your communication, the latter portion of which smacks strongly of the bar. I have written more than was at first designed, and not a word has been dictated by any spirit of unkindness. I only regret that circumstances should have made it necessary to write at all. The argument is at an end.

"Yours truly, ALEX. GREGG.
"Rev. C. GILLETTE."

"AUSTIN, Aug. 15, 1864.

"MY DEAR BISHOP: Your communication of the ninth instant, to which I have been hitherto prevented from replying, I will (D.V.) answer in a few days. I write this morning for another purpose.

"In your note of the fourth instant you say, 'Can no step be taken to prevent more serious disturbance in the Church?' and again: 'I do not wish, even in appearance, to act discourteously, or seem to trample upon what might be considered the rights of others.' In your note of the fifth instant you say: 'My only object and sincere desire is, to do what may promote the Church's welfare, in accordance with the spirit and letter of her laws.'

"I desire respectfully to ask whether, in your judgment, your utter ignoring of me in my official capacity in the administration of the Holy Communion in my church yesterday, was calculated 'to prevent more serious disturbance in the Church'? whether it was, 'in appearance' or in *fact*, courteous? and whether such a course is likely 'to promote the Church's welfare, in accordance with the spirit and letter of her laws'? Your proceeding was so unheard-of, that I am at a loss to know in what light it is to be considered.

"Yours truly, C. GILLETTE.
"Rt. Rev. ALEX. GREGG."

"AUSTIN, Aug. 15, 1864.

"BROTHER GILLETTE: I am not more surprised at its tone than I am at the fact that you should have thought it proper or necessary to make the inquiries contained in your note of this morning; and but for the desire not to wound or give pain where none was intended, would not reply, except to admonish you of your spirit of growing insubordination. My course yesterday as to the Communion was, according to my understanding, but the carrying out, literally, your own invitation for me to 'hold service and preach, ' for the present,' nor did I imagine that *any other* course, under the circumstances, would be expected, or any offense be taken. If there has been any ignoring of your official capacity lately, it has been at your own instance.

"Yours truly, ALEX. GREGG.
"Rev. C. GILLETTE."

"AUSTIN, Aug. 15, 1864.

"MY DEAR BISHOP: I am sorry you seem so far to have misunderstood my note of this morning, and also, in some de-

gree, the relation we hold to each other in this parish. I desired you to have service and preach for me, 'for the present.' By this I understood the usual morning and evening service of the Church on Sundays, with preaching—nothing more, nothing less. When you proposed to me, a week ago, to give notice for the Communion on yesterday, I had no objection, and expected, of course, you would take the leading portion of the Communion service. It is customary for the officiating clergyman on such an occasion to ask a brother who may be with him in the chancel to assist, if not in the prayers, in the administration of the elements. I have never known it otherwise. In my judgment, the circumstances made it highly proper that you should have done this yesterday. I thought so then, and think so still; and I think unbiased men who understand the case will agree with me. I have not intended to give my parish into your hands beyond the ordinary service of every Sunday, and I supposed you would have so understood it. I can assure you my questions were propounded in no spirit of insubordination, but because I thought there had been a violation of the common courtesies of brethren, which it would be better to avoid. I am glad to learn from you that there was no intention to wound or give pain. Still, it is but right and just to tell you plainly, that you did wound and give great pain, not only to myself, but to numbers of the communicants. Yours truly, CHARLES GILLETTE.
"Rt. Rev. ALEX. GREGG."

"AUSTIN, Aug. 15, 1864.
"BROTHER GILLETTE: I will now say what I might have added to my note of this morning but for the want of time. You speak of replying to my last communication in a few days. This will be unnecessary, as the correspondence is at an end. For enough has been said, the argument is virtually exhausted, and I can see nothing good to result from an indulgence in personal reflections, to which any thing further would be calculated to lead. *Besides,* the *tone* of your last, of the second instant, as well as your note of to-day, is such as to forbid my receiving any further communication from you, unless with the assurance that it is written in a proper strain.

I am impelled to this course by motives of duty and propriety alike, and, as your Bishop, will only add *one warning word* to you in conclusion, and *that is*, to weigh well the course upon which you have entered, as it only seems to be leading you, in spirit, from one degree of insubordination to another.

"Yours in the Church, ALEX GREGG.
"Rev. C. GILLETTE.

"P. S.—Just as I was about to send this off, your note of this afternoon was handed to me. It calls, however, for no reply. A. G."

To the foregoing note I made no reply at the time. Perhaps none was necessary, either then or at a later period. Taken in connection with the preceding correspondence, it probably carries along with it its own refutation, and shows as clearly the working of the Bishop's mind without as it would with comment. The following communication I had partially prepared before receiving the Bishop's note, as above. But as he forbid my sending it to him, I did not complete it until since the close of our civil war.

"AUSTIN, August 10, 1864.

"MY DEAR BISHOP: Although you announce, in a somewhat peremptory manner, that the argument is at an end, yet you will no doubt permit me a few words in reply.

"I can by no means allow your clear and indisputable point. For however it may be to you, it is by no means 'clear and indisputable' to me.

"How could you overlook the language of the Constitution, 'no alteration or addition,' and substitute your italicized words '*any change*,' and then base your argument upon the Prayer-Book's being left intact by your prayers?—that because your prayers are not inserted within the book, therefore it is no violation of the Constitution of the Church? Your principle of reasoning, if correct, would allow a Bishop to put forth an entire service for the Church, and compel his clergy to use it on 'all occasions of public worship,' and if he did not have it bound up in the same volume with the Book of Common Prayer, it would be no violation of the law of the Church.

For in such a case, it would 'form no more a part of the Prayer-Book, than of the building' in which the prayers were used. But I know you will not allow your own argument when carried out legitimately. Let us not distract by making false issues. The plain object of the Eighth Article and Twentieth Canon, is to regulate public worship in the Church, by enjoining 'the use of the prayers in the Book of Common Prayer, and no others.' In this sense, which is the plain and obvious meaning of the language of the law, the constant use of your prayers is as much an 'alteration,' and 'addition' to the Prayer-Book, as much so as if they were inserted in the book itself. Again, why attempt to draw the mind away from the point at issue, by talking about the illegality of a Council's putting forth prayers? No one claims that it would be lawful for a council to put forth prayers, even for an extraordinary occasion. In reasoning upon the Twentieth Canon, why attempt to confuse by talking about a clergyman or bishop using unauthorized prayers? Why talk of the Council, Diocesan or General, issuing prayers for permanent use? What has our argument to do with all this, unless you wish to distract, and draw away the mind from the point in question? Why assume the point upon which the question turns, and try to make it hinge upon something foreign to the subject, and about which nothing has been said? The question is simple. Do the laws of the Church authorize a Bishop to put forth prayers for an extraordinary occasion, which shall embrace an indefinite period—for a series of years—it may be for a generation, and compel his clergy to incorporate these into the public worship of the Church 'on all occasions'? I can not so understand it. Nor can I understand that the Eighth Article of the Constitution, and Twentieth Canon, have nothing to do in regulating the setting forth Special Prayers for continued use in the Church.

"I do not assert that the prayers in question constitute a leaf within the lids of the Prayer-Book, nor can I suppose that is all the Article and Canon are intended to cover. But rather to prevent 'alterations or additions' to the forms of Church service in constant use. Now the two prayers in question add to the daily or weekly liturgy of the Church, just as much as if they were inserted in the morning and evening service, and this they have done on all occasions of public worship for several years; and if your assertion is correct, may continue to do for a generation to come, for who can tell when this war will end? If extraordinary occasions can be made to cover 'all occasions' of public worship for a series of years, and that too, when the Church has provided her own prayers, how easy for Bishops to make all occasions for which the Church has provided Special Prayers, 'extraordinary occasions,' and so give us, under one or other of these occasions, their prayers continually? For if they have a right to set aside a prayer of the Church, and substitute theirs in one case, they have in any or all cases provided for by the Church, and so there would be constant and increasing additions to the form of public worship, which is, to all intents and purposes, adding to the Book of Common Prayer, and ministers would never have an occasion when they would use the prayers of that book and no other.

"I am surprised at what looks like a simple quibble in your argument about the addition to the Prayer-Book. No one supposes your prayers are within the lids of the Book of Common Prayer. No one supposes the law of the Church confined to such an addition.

"Whether this matter can be made clearer by argument or not, the conclusions we arrive at are widely different. Your mode of disposing of the Eighth Article, and the Twentieth Canon, looks as if you found it much easier to cut than untie the knot.

"You seem not to have observed my language in regard to your second deduction from Dr. Hawks, neither the manner in which the Doctor uses the word 'period.'

"I said it was not a period in the sense of which we were speaking, namely, a continuous period, covering 'all occasions of public worship,' but simply a single service occurring annually. You quote Dr. Hawks's language thus, 'When the Church *has* provided a service, we think it would be best not to deem the period appointed for its use, an extraordinary occasion,' and you triumphantly ask, 'in the name of logic, and common-sense, what does this mean, if not in Dr. Hawks's view, where no service is provided, an "extraordinary occasion" may be for a period?' If you will allow an honest answer to this question, to settle the matter, then the argument to this part of the subject will indeed be 'at an end,' and you must own yourself vanquished, for it settles the meaning of 'extraordinary occasion,' to be only a simple service, and not a continuous time. The 'period' of which Dr. Hawks speaks, is only a single service, happening once a year; and it can be made to cover only this one service. Hence your 'extraordinary occasion,' unprovided for by the Church, and for which a Bishop may put forth a Special Prayer, must also be a 'period' of one service only.

"I have again examined your language in regard to my responsibility in using the prayers in question, as set forth in your communication of July twenty-second. I understand you to refer to my responsibility in using the prayers, and not yours in putting them forth. That although I may think there was a violation of the law of the Church, yet you intimate to me that I am to have no conscience in the matter. You are to order, I am to obey, and with you rests the responsibility. This seems to me a short way of expressing your idea, as contained in your language. Your letter was published, and I think many besides myself understood you as saying about what I expressed. Your reasoning might appear better on this subject, if your assumption, that you have ordered and insisted on nothing contrary to law, were true. But you have assumed the very point in dispute. I contend you have ordered that which is contrary to Canon, and the question is, when a superior orders an inferior to break what he believes a plain law, may he (the inferior) obey and be guiltless? I must repeat, I do not know any such doctrine of shifting responsibility. You certainly have a very singular way of putting the case when taken in connection with what you now say you meant. You are speaking of 'the canonical propriety of special prayers like those in use here for a Time of War,' (and this 'canonical propriety,' involves the use of them by the clergyman. You say: 'You are not responsible in the case at all. The Bishop has to bear that; and no one would imagine, that should he have erred in judgment, any guilt in such a case would be incurred.' It might not be amiss to ask here, how much greater is the guilt of a Presbyter for erring in judgment, than that of a Bishop? I think your argument would go to show that the guilt of the Presbyter consists in his exercising his judgment. He must have none, in this respect at least, except as he gets it from his Bishop.

"I do not know that I am called upon to follow you through your answer, in which you seem to have lost your temper, and to make use of language which carries with it its own refutation. My desire in this discussion has been to arrive at truth in connection with the Canon law of the Church. I did think, and I still think, I have a right to an opinion on the subject. If I am wrong, I have no objection to defer to the voice of the Church. If your opinion is correct, then the law of the Church needs revision, to make it explicit and harmonious, so that in future there may be no misunderstanding.

"I will now, for the present at least, leave the question of Canon law, and discuss the more serious case of conscience, in connection with your attempt to compel me to use the words, 'which has been forced upon us,' in your Special Prayer. I contend you have exceeded your authority as a Bishop in the Church of God; that you have violated the law of charity—and that you have set at naught the great principle of the Protestant reformation.

"I told you in the very outset, that the words, 'which has been forced upon us,' in the prayer put forth, asserted, as a matter of fact, what I believed to be false. Your intention was to assert, that this was forced upon the South by the North. This you and the Council assert to be 'an historical fact.' This I do not, and never have believed. On the contrary, so far as I have been able to gather facts, from what I saw and heard passing around me, I think the South threatened war first, and finally chose it and commenced it, as a way of deciding a political difference. I do not stop here to adduce reasons for this opinion. I simply state it to be my opinion. To this opinion, formed from the best data of information I could get, I had a right, and neither you, nor the Council, had any right, individually or officially, to deprive me of it, or force me to abjure it, by compelling me publicly to declare to the contrary, and least of all, in a solemn, public act of worship to Almighty God.

"So far as the argument goes, it matters not whether I was correct in my opinion or not, if I sincerely believed the assertion false. You were bound to respect my conscientious scruples, and not try to compel me, week after week, to utter before God, that which I believed to be false. For three years you respected my conscientious scruple, and during that time you told me you thought you were right in so doing—you then, without one word of previous intimation that you had changed your mind, withdrew your permission, and compelled me to do one of two things, either to violate my conscience, or to cease to officiate. Of course, I chose the latter alternative. In doing this, you plainly exceeded your authority as a Bishop. No Bishop has a right to exercise an authority over the conscience of one of his Presbyters, or even one of the Laity. The Church has nowhere given such authority to her Bishops, an authority which would be anti-protestant and unscriptural.

"*But, again*, if the matter of Canon law be waived, and it be granted you have a right to put forth prayers to be used by your clergy for a series of years, (which I do not believe,) still you must conform to the law of the Church in framing those prayers. Her law is her usage. In her public prayers she does not insert political opinions, or declare 'historical facts.' Judged by her standard, you exceeded your authority as a Bishop in the house of God. When a Bishop has violated her rule, although he may have done it thoughtlessly, one would suppose it a plain matter of duty on his part when his attention was called to the fact, to erase the obnoxious clause, rather than attempt to compel his clergy to use it, and so violate their conscience.

"Again, in the enforcement of the use of a prayer put forth by a Bishop, he is to follow the rule of the Church in like cases, which is to respect conscientious scruples. If she has no written law upon the subject, she has her own usage, which has the force of written law. See how carefully she deals with conscience even in her solemn creed; she directs that any minister, or any congregation having scruples in regard to the words, 'He descended into hell,' may substitute others, or omit them altogether. In the administration of Holy Baptism, she directs that, any parents or sponsors desiring it, the minister officiating may omit the sign of the cross, and the words accompanying. All this yielding on her part, is to scruples of conscience, and she yields it, too, without any upbraidings, or attempts at wit or sarcasm, thrown out against her children who have these scruples. Has the enforcement of your prayer been according to her rule? By violating her custom, her universal practice, so far as the reformed Catholic Church is concerned, have you not exceeded your authority in the Church of God?

"Your opinion, in the prayer, is a mere political opinion, or as you and the council term it, 'an historical fact;' and it is introduced as mere assertion, as if it were necessary in public worship to inform the Almighty of, 'historical facts.' To leave it out, takes no petition from the prayer. To assert it or not, affects no religious truth. When first introduced, it was disbelieved by a number of your clergy and many of the laity in your diocese; numbers of the latter of whom have never said Amen to it, and never would, if it was to continue in use for the term of their natural life. Numbers in my own congregation, who have been the warmest friends of the Church, and the supporters of this congregation for years, did not believe it, and would not say Amen to it. All this was known to you before you attempted to compel me to violate my conscience in uttering what I believed untrue; and yet you persisted in your course, and compelled me, through public excitement, to resign my parish. You refused to assist in reading the prayers—as you had voluntarily done for years—and thus relieve me from that part of the service in which your prayer occurred. You would not appoint a lay-reader to assist me, who might do the same in your absence. Yet you did not hesitate to appoint such a reader, who should take the whole service, and read a sermon while I sat in the congregation, (whether such a proceeding be a violation of Canon law, let the proper authorities judge.) You did all you could to ignore me in my ministerial capacity, not only not allowing me to assist in the service, or to preach in my own church, when you had compelled me to invite you to hold service, but you proceeded to administer the communion to my congregation, while I was sitting in the chancel with my surplice on, not even allowing me the place of a deacon to administer the cup. Several of the communicants who did not go forward at first, were so wounded by this act, as to stay away from the communion, and others who went forward first, would not have gone, if they had dreamed what you intended to do. Has not such conduct, on your part, been a gross violation of Christian charity? What was my offense, for which you chose, in this and other instances, (without a charge against me, or the possibility of a charge being brought,) to publicly intimate to the congregation, that I had no right to minister in holy things? Simply that I did not, in a solemn prayer to God, at your bidding, make an assertion which I conscientiously believed to be untrue. What Pope of Rome ever required greater obedience to his infallible mandate? Was not freedom of conscience one of the main points contended for in the Reformation? Must we now, three hundred years after the fighting of that great battle for religious liberty, have—what? Not an article of faith pertaining to religion, not a declaration in regard to a truth of the Gospel, or that which in any way pertains to revealed truth, but simply a political opinion, pronounced by the council an 'historical fact,' placed in a special prayer, and made a part of the Liturgy of the Church for years, and the clergyman who can not adopt it as a part of his faith, or will not do violence to his conscience by uttering a falsehood as often as he officiates in the Church, must be debarred from officiating, and driven from his church! Is not such a course stripping us of the great boon of the Reformation—liberty of conscience? If an infuriated atheistic mob had done such a deed in this the nineteenth century, to carry a point in infidelity, or political intrigue, it would scarcely have been credited. Who, then, will believe that a Christian Bishop, in his paternal care, with his great love for the souls of men, and to whom 'the reputation of his clergy is very dear,' has so far forgotten the duties of his high station, as to mete out such vengeance to one of his clergy, for no other reason than that he happens to differ from his Bishop in a political opinion?

"There are other points which have arisen in the course of this discussion, which it may be well to refer to.

"It has been urged by yourself and others, that omitting the words 'which has been forced upon us,' the unity of worship is destroyed. The Church herself has never sought to enforce any such unity as is thus referred to—a verbal uniformity in every congregation throughout a diocese.

"This appears from her direction in regard to the use of the Creed and the Baptismal service. It also appears from the very Canon by which a bishop is authorized to put forth a prayer for an 'extraordinary occasion.'

"The Church knows of no uniformity of worship by Dioceses. Her uniformity, so far as sought, is sought for an entire branch of the Church. Yet, even here, she neither desires nor enjoins any such uniformity as that for which you contend. Her 'occasional prayers and thanksgivings,' set forth to be used according to the discretion of each clergyman, or the necessities of his congregation, make constant change and variation, and keep the uniformity here spoken of. The permission for clergymen in any diocese or territory where there is no bishop, to select any prayer put forth by any bishop for an extraordinary occasion, gives license for as many different prayers within a diocese, on any specified 'extraordinary occasion,' as there are clergy in the diocese.

"But your own course shows that the plea for uniformity had in reality no weight in your own mind; but was simply a plea by which to oppress one who differed from you politically. For had uniformity been really what you sought, you would not have pursued the course you have. For instance, your desire for uniformity is so great, that you can not allow one of your clergy to omit six declaratory words in a prayer you have put forth. Yet you kindly give the same clergyman the gratuitous information that he is at liberty to use the prayer set forth by the Church for 'times of war and tumult,' in addition to those set forth by yourself, while you neither use that prayer yourself, nor direct your clergy generally to use it. In other words, in your opinion, the introduction and constant use by one of your clergy of an entire prayer, used by none of the others in the diocese, or by yourself, would conduce more to uniformity in worship, than the omission of six words by one of your clergy, in a prayer put forth by yourself, and these words containing no petition.

"Again, you debar a clergyman from officiating, because he can not conscientiously use six words in your prayer; and for months you place a lay-reader in the congregation, the charge of which you have compelled the clergyman to resign. Yet this lay-reader cannot pronounce the absolution, or the greater benediction—never reads the ante-communion service, (which most, if not all of your clergy do.) He can not baptize, nor administer the communion, yet he can read the six words in your prayer. Does this, in your estimation, constitute uniformity of worship? Your lay-reader can do all this, while a presbyter sits in the congregation, laboring under no 'disability,' except that which you have imposed upon him, by bidding him assert in prayer, an opinion which he believes untrue. What shall we say of such consistent labors to produce uniformity in the service of the Church?

"This whole matter may now be summed up in few words. It is evident, from all our correspondence, that my offense (very grievous in your eyes) has been, that I did not sympathize so deeply with the Southern Confederacy, as you thought I ought to do. I suppose you felt like many others, that you had staked every thing upon its success, and you were unwilling that any one over whom you had any influence or authority, should do otherwise. Acting upon your theory, that 'the Church and State are now, and ever will be, closely and indissolubly connected,' you conceived that you were authorized to put forth a political test in the Church, and bring all to your standard of thinking in matters of state. This idea seems to me to have been the radical stone of error, upon which you built all your assumption and persecution, claiming the right to control my conscience in matters where you have not, and by right never could have, any control.

"Because I would not yield a blind submission, you took advantage of the excited state of men's minds, and placed me in a position where, I understand, according to your own assertion, you had to interfere to save my life. Be this as it may, it is very certain you would not dare to pursue any such course of persecution in times of peace and quiet. It would not have been prudent for me to have written thus to you six months ago. But times have now changed, and men who for years have been compelled to be silent, or speak according to a rule prescribed by others, can now talk without fear.

"Before dismissing this subject, let us ask how will this record sound in the future history of the Church—a record which shall transmit to posterity the fact, that a bishop of the Church considered the assertion of a political opinion in prayer to God, of more importance than all the prayers of the Church and the preaching of the Gospel?—that men who could not assert the politics of their bishop, must be silenced from the ministry for the time being? Will the people of Christendom believe a thing so strange? Will they believe that under any circumstances, there could have been such infatuation?—that a minister of the Gospel should be forbidden to preach, and deprived of his church by a Christian bishop, because he could not tell the Almighty that a certain political opinion of his bishop was true, when he believed it false? How does all this compare with the teaching and example of the blessed Jesus? Has all this been according to His Gospel?"

"MY DEAR BISHOP: I had expected to say to you, previous to your leaving Austin, what I now write. The opportunity not offering, I take this mode of informing you that I am just on the eve of my departure for the North, where I expect (D. V.) to have some facts in connection with the Church in Texas, together with our correspondence, published. As you would not permit me to send you my closing communications, I add them in the publication. Should you desire to continue this correspondence publicly, I shall hold myself in readiness to answer any communication you may address to me. So far as the Canons and Constitution of the Church are concerned, I shall use my best endeavors to have the points at issue definitely settled by the General Convention. I hope it may be your pleasure to be present, that you may aid in the settlement of so important a matter.

"Yours truly, CHARLES GILLETTE.
"AUSTIN, August 31, 1865."

www.ingramcontent.com/pod-product-compliance
Lightning Source LLC
Chambersburg PA
CBHW022135160426
43197CB00009B/1301